THE POLITICS OF DEBT IN ARGENTINA, BRAZIL & MEXICO

RESEARCH SERIES/NUMBER 72

The POLITICS OF DEBT in Argentina, Brazil, and Mexico

Economic Stabilization in the 1980s

ROBERT R. KAUFMAN

iiS

INSTITUTE
OF INTERNATIONAL
STUDIES
University of California, Berkeley

Library of Congress Cataloging-in-Publication Data

Kaufman, Robert R.
The politics of debt in Argentina, Brazil & Mexico.

(Research series, ISSN 0068-6093 ; no. 72)
Bibliography: p.
1. Debts, External—Latin America —Case studies.
2. Economic stabilization—Latin America—Case studies.
3. Latin America—Economic conditions—1982- .
4. Mexico—Economic conditions—1982- .
5. Argentina—Economic conditions—1983- .
6. Brazil—Economic conditions—1985- .
I. Title. II. Series: Research series (University of California, Berkeley. Institute of International Studies) ; no. 72.
HJ8514.5.K38 1988 336.3'435'098 88-32792
ISBN 0-87725-172-X

CONTENTS

LIST OF TABLES/FIGURES

ACKNOWLEDGMENTS

This book has emerged from an ongoing collaborative research project on the Politics of Stabilization and Adjustment, funded jointly by the Ford Foundation and the Rockefeller Foundation. For their support, criticisms, and suggestions, I would like to thank my collaborators on this larger project: Thomas Callaghy, Stephan Haggard, Miles Kahler, Joan Nelson, and Barbara Stallings. The manuscript also benefitted from suggestions by David and Ruth Collier, Eric Davis, Cheryl Eschbach, from the creative editing of Paul Gilchrist, and from the criticisms of participants in seminars held at El Colegio de México, Columbia University, the Kellogg Institute at the University of Notre Dame, Rutgers, and UCLA. Todd Appel and Nancy Llach provided able research assistance. Finally, for this book as well as for many other good things, I owe a huge debt to my wife, Laura Schoen, who meets exceptionally high standards of excellence in her own career, yet somehow finds the energy to provide love and encouragement for me. Both her example and her encouragement have undoubtedly inspired me to work much harder than I would otherwise have done.

R. R. K.

INTRODUCTION

Whatever their disagreements about the causes and consequences of the economic shocks of the 1980s, the historians of future decades are almost certain to agree that the "debt crisis" marked a watershed of major proportions in Latin America. In the United States, the most salient aspect of this crisis has been the threat it has posed to the solvency of the international financial system—hardly a trivial concern, and one that vitally affects Latin America as well. Yet for Latin Americans, the crisis has had an even more immediate and far-reaching impact. The sudden interruption of access to the private international credit market—a fact of life since the early 1980s—has already forced extraordinarily painful economic adjustments in terms of reduced imports, severe recessions, and a substantial transfer of resources abroad. And in the majority of countries, the crisis has had major political repercussions as well. It has contributed to the collapse of military governments, posed threats to the stability of constitutional regimes, and stimulated wide debates almost everywhere about what kinds of adjustment strategies should be adopted and who should pay the costs.

The two sets of policy studies presented in this volume are meant to be read against the backdrop of this larger panorama of international and regional developments. The first study provides a close-in description of "heterodox" efforts to control inflation in Argentina and Brazil during the mid-1980s; the second offers analysis and political interpretation of more "orthodox" policies in Mexico. Although both of these discussions are set in larger historical-structural contexts, neither purports to cover in depth the full range of challenges that have emerged during the current decade. The essays are, however, relevant to a broader understanding of these challenges in at least three important ways.

First, economic stabilization is an important component of the broad agenda of policy issues confronting Latin American governments. Conventionally the economic objectives at stake in stabilization policies (i.e., the management of inflation and current accounts deficits) have been distinguished analytically from structural adjustment issues (such as trade liberalization or reform of the public enterprise sector), which are presumed to deal more broadly with the overall organization of the economy and its capacity to expand over the longer term. While such distinctions may be useful, stabilization *per se* has always been a difficult problem for Latin American governments and has posed especially hard choices since 1982. On the one hand, private banks and other creditor agencies have attempted to make monetary and fiscal orthodoxy a condition of debt rescheduling and other forms of external financial assistance. On the other hand, whether or not the governments of the region have chosen to comply with such demands, they have had to find ways to allocate the costs of austerity among competing domestic groups. The manner in which a government responds to such a dilemma must be considered an important aspect of its capacity to deal with the crisis as a whole.

In the second place, these studies provide a useful vantage point from which to observe the types of linkages that are perceived between stabilization objectives and broad recovery strategies. What causal connections do governments see between, say, external debt servicing, domestic fiscal deficits, and control of inflation? What are the implications for the kinds of bargaining stances to be adopted with external creditors? Stabilization invariably leads political actors and observers alike into consideration of these other issues. Yet as we shall see below, governments have defined the connections in a variety of ways—or at times have ignored them entirely. In this respect, the focus on stabilization policy begins to direct attention to variations in the way the broader crisis itself has been defined and to the kinds of strategies aimed at coping with it.

Finally, as has been true throughout the postwar period, stabilization policies touch a wide range of political interests and institutions, and an analysis of stabilization thus opens a window on these relations and offers an opportunity to explore how they interact with the policies selected. In what ways were the experimental approaches in Argentina and Brazil shaped by their transitions toward constitutional democracy? What aspects of Mexico's dominant one-party system contributed to contrasting policy choices in Mexico? What sorts of consequences can we expect for each society?

In our exploration of these issues, two broad sets of assumptions will serve as points of departure. The first set concerns the room for maneuver that is available to Latin American governments within the overall framework of North-South power relations. In important respects the crisis of the 1980s has again revealed the extraordinary asymmetry of these relations. Creditor governments, private banks, and multinational lenders have all been able to coordinate their bargaining positions to a considerable extent—concentrating their attention on the issue of debt rescheduling and Latin American economic adjustments. Latin American governments, in contrast, have been induced or compelled to confront their creditors separately, and they have little leverage over creditor-country trade, monetary, and fiscal policies that vitally affect their capacity to pay. As long as such issues are left off the agenda—as long as the Latin Americans cannot insist, say, that the United States cut its fiscal deficit or open its markets to Latin American exports—it is unlikely that they will be able to shift much of the costs of adjustment abroad.

I assume, however, that even within this constricted international framework, the larger Latin American debtors have had opportunities to choose among a fairly wide variety of external bargaining strategies and domestic policy positions. Argentina, Brazil, and Mexico—the three largest—have been in a good position to extract rescheduling concessions from creditors by posing threats to the solvency of the international financial system (Haggard and Kaufman 1987; Bogdaniwicz-Bindert 1985). Moreover, as it has become increasingly clear that not even "good debtors" can expect a rapid resumption of international credit, a growing number of governments have begun to consider previously "unthinkable" options for unilaterally reducing their debt servicing obligations. In this context, even highly orthodox creditor institutions such as the International Monetary Fund (IMF) have been compelled to adopt somewhat more flexible stances toward experimentation with domestic stabilization policies.

The second set of assumptions concerns the comparability of the countries that have wrestled with such policies. We focus here on concurrent policy developments in Argentina, Brazil, and Mexico (the "ABM countries"), but it must be conceded at the outset that these are quite divergent societies. Differences in petroleum resources—Mexico exports oil and Brazil imports it—is only one of the many points of divergence. Another possibly more important one is in the choice of development models adopted during the 1970s: the neo-conservative policies pursued in Argentina from 1976-83 led in very different directions from the state-sponsored industrialization policies adopted in Brazil and Mexico. Such choices, as we shall see below, left quite distinctive legacies for the governments charged with dealing with the debt problems of the 1980s.

Despite these differences, however, there are some broad parallels which provide a basis for comparative analysis. The ABM countries—in addition to being the three largest debtors in Latin America—also had the largest economies as measured in terms of gross domestic product (GDP) and industrial development. Although their developmental paths began to diverge after the mid-1970s, earlier patterns ran along similar lines: all three experienced accelerated import-substitution in the 1930s and 1940s, all began to attract foreign manufacturing investment in the 1950s, and all turned toward investment in capital goods and manufactured exports in the late 1960s and early 1970s.* In Brazil and Argentina, the parallels extended into the political sphere as well. In both countries the postwar period was marked by the rise and fall of fragile civilian governments, by highly politicized military institutions, and by prolonged periods of authoritarian rule. In the mid-1980s both countries also began transitions in the direction of more democratic regimes.

The comparisons undertaken within this context will serve two analytic purposes (Skocpol 1984). The first is to highlight some of the distinctive aspects of the politico-institutional forces operating in each country by mapping contrasts among the three cases. Several themes in the first chapter on Argentina and Brazil reflect this concern. Roughly equivalent historical rates of inflation in the two countries masked quite different underlying patterns of distributive politics, and the heterodox anti-inflation packages introduced in the mid-1980s had quite different kinds of political and economic impacts. These contrasts provide a useful context for gauging the dimensions and possible consequences of the more orthodox policies implemented in Mexico.

Comparisons will also be used to explore the kinds of political and institutional forces that appear most relevant to cross-national variations in responses to the crisis of the 1980s. For this purpose the parallels among the ABM countries can serve as a common ground for discussing how policies can be shaped by a variety of factors:

*For references on development patterns in Argentina, see Diaz-Alejandro (1970), Mallon and Sourrouille (1975), Randall (1978), and Villaneuva (1966); for Brazil, see Bergsman (1970), Baer (1965), Leff (1968), Suzigan et al. (1974), and Kahil (1973); for Mexico, see King (1970), Hansen (1971), and Hewlett and Weinert (1982).

political regimes, bureaucratic organization, interest-group conflict, etc. Much of this analytic material is embedded in the historically specific, highly context-bound "policy stories" related about the ABM countries, but it is hoped that some of the causal connections suggested by these stories will be helpful in understanding other countries as well. Some of the hypotheses sketched in the final chapter will be tentative steps in that direction.

Inductive research cannot be undertaken without theoretical assumptions and predispositions. In this connection many readers are almost certain to detect the influence of a number of broad conceptual perspectives on the organization and presentation of the historical material. Perhaps the most conventional is the assumption that policy outcomes reflect the power relations among contending sociopolitical interests—an emphasis which directs attention to the structuring of sociopolitical conflicts and coalitions within civil society and abroad (Gourevitch 1986). A second useful perspective is provided by the "state capacity" literature (e.g., Zysman 1983). This focuses principally on the goals and interests of state elites and on their command over resources which might enable them to reorient the behavior of domestic and external political actors. Third, the analysis applies the Marxist insight that private control over investment resources constrains the behavior of both state elites and other social actors (Poulantzas 1978; O'Conner 1973; Lindblom 1977). Our understanding of this constraint is still very incomplete, but in the debt crisis it appears to have played an important role in the "accumulation/legitimation" dilemmas endemic in the region.

These issues are important, but the primary purpose of this study is to provide a preliminary glimpse of important policy processes in rapidly changing political environments. Since the structural and institutional parameters are unstable, much of the description and analysis of the policy processes must be tentative, and it is largely for that reason that I have not attempted to squeeze my presentation into preconceived categories. One price paid for this, perhaps, is that too much analysis may lie buried in the description, left for readers to uncover for themselves. On the other hand, with a longer time perspective, we will almost certainly be able to sort through these events and assess their significance with greater confidence than is now possible. In this respect, a relatively open-ended account of events may reveal a few useful pieces of the larger puzzle.

Chapter One

THE POLITICS OF INFLATION IN ARGENTINA AND BRAZIL: THE AUSTRAL AND THE CRUZADO

The problem of inflation is by no means a new one in Argentina and Brazil. Throughout the post-1945 era the economies of these two countries have been among the most inflationary in the world (see Table 1). In the 1950s annual price increases averaged around 20 percent—modest by today's standards, but well above the regional averages of the time. In subsequent decades, triple-digit inflations were not uncommon. They plagued both the authoritarian and the democratic regimes that alternated in power throughout the 1960s and 1970s. By the 1980s, in the context of oil, debt, and interest-rate shocks, serious concern about escalation toward hyperinflation was one of the main economic challenges confronting the constitutional governments of Raul Alfonsín in Argentina and José Sarney in Brazil.

In this chapter we shall examine the politics of two recent "heterodox" attempts to deal with problems of inflation—the Austral program decreed under Alfonsín in June 1985 and the Cruzado program decreed under Sarney in February 1986.* In contrast to more orthodox demand-management approaches to price stabilization advocated by the IMF, these programs focused on the inertial components of the inflationary spirals and on the need to break such spirals directly through the implementation of currency reforms and price controls. Thus, at a time when Mexico and many other countries were wrestling with more conventional forms of fiscal and monetary austerity, the Argentine and Brazilian initiatives were attracting substantial international attention as possible alternatives to more "recessive" approaches.

Despite initial parallels, however, the two programs eventually led in significantly different directions. After a brief but intense

*Each program is named after the new currency issued under it.

Table 1

Annual Rates of Growth and Inflation in Argentina and Brazil, 1946–1986
(In percent)

Year	Argentina Growth of GDP	Argentina Inflation[a]	Brazil Growth of GDP	Brazil Inflation[b]
1946	–	17.1%	–	27.3%
1947	–	12.2	–	5.8
1948	–	13.0	7.4%	3.5
1949	–	32.7	6.6	6.0
1950	–	24.6	6.5	11.4
1951	3.8%	37.2	6.0	10.8
1952	-5.0	38.1	8.7	20.4
1953	5.4	4.3	2.5	17.6
1954	4.1	3.5	10.1	25.6
1955	7.1	12.5	6.9	18.9
1956	2.8	13.1	3.2	21.8
1957	5.1	25.0	8.1	13.4
1958	6.3	31.4	7.7	17.3
1959	-6.4	113.9	5.6	51.9
1960	7.9	27.3	9.7	23.8
1961	7.1	13.5	10.3	42.9
1962	-1.7	28.1	5.3	51.6
1963	-2.4	24.0	1.5	75.4
1964	10.4	22.1	2.9	90.5
1965	9.1	28.6	2.7	56.8
1966	0.7	31.9	5.1	37.9
1967	2.6	29.2	4.8	28.4
1968	4.6	16.2	9.2	24.2
1969	7.9	7.6	9.0	20.8
1970	4.1	13.6	8.3	19.8
1971	3.7	39.1	12.0	21.4
1972	1.9	64.1	11.1	17.7
1973	3.5	43.8	13.6	15.5
1974	5.7	40.2	9.7	35.4
1975	-0.4	335.1	5.4	27.8
1976	-0.5	347.5	9.7	40.4
1977	6.4	160.4	5.7	40.6
1978	-3.4	169.8	5.0	38.9
1979	6.7	139.7	6.4	55.4
1980	0.7	87.6	7.2	109.2
1981	-6.2	131.3	-1.6	113.0
1982	-4.6	209.7	0.9	94.0
1983	2.8	433.7	-3.2	164.9
1984	2.6	688.0	4.5	232.9
1985	-4.5	385.0	8.3	223.3
1986	5.7	81.9	8.2	58.4

Sources: Argentina: 1946-70—Skidmore (1977: 150, 166); 1971-86—Dornbusch and De Pablo (1987: 27). Brazil: 1946-61—Skidmore (1977: 150, 170); 1962-86—Cardoso and Fishlow (1987: 90, 101).

[a] 1946–70: rise in cost of living; 1971–86: increase in consumer prices.

[b] 1946–61: rise in cost of living; 1962–86: rise in wholesale price index.

honeymoon period of about nine months, Brazil's Cruzado program, which placed an especially high priority on distributive and expansionary objectives, began to come apart suddenly at the end of 1986. By 1987-88 the Sarney administration faced inflationary pressures even more severe than in the pre-Cruzado period, together with a deepening economic recession. The Argentine government, though not without major disappointments, fared better. The Austral program, which combined price controls with conventional adjustments on the fiscal and monetary side, produced significantly lower rates of inflation for several years. Although the Alfonsín administration was unable to follow through with fundamental trade and fiscal reforms (which eventually eroded some of its anti-inflationary achievements), Argentine policymakers did show a substantial capacity to fend off a stabilization crisis that threatened to undermine a still fragile democratic transition.

In the following pages we will examine closely how the Alfonsín and Sarney governments came to adopt their important new initiatives, and why they had such divergent outcomes. Underlying this examination is a larger set of issues:

What are the connections between these particular kinds of stabilization programs and the emergence of new democracies?

To what extent are we simply witnessing a repetition of past political-economic cycles?

What elements of the current situation suggest the possibility of new long-term directions?

Our analysis of these issues is organized into three sections. The first provides a broad overview of the historical experiences with inflation and stabilization in order to highlight some of the principal variables relevant to an understanding of the current situation. The second section describes the initiation of the Austral and Cruzado programs and their implementation over the course of the first one or two years. In the third section we focus on the ways in which patterns of implementation were altered by changing relations between the government and the majority party, economic interest-groups, and the international environment.

Before proceeding further, we must add another important assumption to those already noted in the Introduction. The assumption is that it is neither necessary nor useful to stake out a firm position with respect to the debates among economists about the emphasis and design of competing policy packages. On the one hand, after many decades of unsuccessful anti-inflationary experiments, divisions among economists are far more fluid and complex than they were in the "monetarist/structuralist" debates of the 1950s (Hirschman 1961; Baer and Kerstenetzky 1964). By the 1980s even relatively orthodox economists often attributed substantial importance to factors not easily brought under control by demand-management instruments alone—for example, the fiscal pressures associated with external debt servicing and the periodic inertial adjustments of wages and prices (see Eshag and Thorp 1965; Thorp and Whitehead 1979; Foxley 1980; Foxley and Whitehead 1980; Wynia 1978; O'Donnell and Frenkel 1974; Williamson 1985; Fishlow 1985; Diamand 1978). On the other hand, most contemporary explanations of inflation assign at least some role to the kinds of fiscal and monetary imbalances emphasized in conventional neoclassical approaches. In the context of these converging analytic opinions, it does not seem inappropriate to remain neutral about the relative weights assigned to such factors in the discussion of specific inflationary situations. Instead, for our purposes, it seems best to leave such issues to the economists.

At the same time, as Albert Hirschman has suggested, "It would be difficult to find an economist who would not agree that underlying social and political forces play a decisive role in causing both inflation and the success or failure of anti-inflationary policies" (1985: 53). Examination of these forces offers relatively secure footing for the political scientist. In this chapter, accordingly, the primary focus is on distributive conflicts at work in Argentina and Brazil and the resources and interests of the new constitutional officials who must deal with these conflicts.

Historical Profiles of Inflation and Stabilization

Under what conditions have inflationary pressures become salient to state authorities in Argentina and Brazil, and what institutional and political pressures determine the kinds of choices they have made? Figure 1 summarizes the principal cross-national patterns of distributive conflicts to be discussed. In Argentina, recurrent cycles of inflation and orthodox stabilization have tended historically to reflect zero-sum conflicts among evenly balanced domestic class and sectoral forces and tense confrontations with international investment forces abroad. For the first several decades after World War II, these conflicts frustrated the sustained implementation of either state-

Figure 1

STABILIZATION/INFLATION PROFILES IN BRAZIL AND ARGENTINA

Key Variables	Argentina	Brazil
Class/sectoral conflict	High conflict; linked to Peron period of 1943-49	Moderate conflict; linked to Vargas period; greater intensity about 1960
Access to external financing	Problematic; funding more limited than Brazil	Excellent access, especially in late 1950s and from 1967 to 1981; provides important basis for industrial development
Relations between state and business	Argentine export and industrial sectors develop low tolerance for price instability; preference for liquid capital and short investment time horizons	Brazilian business establishes close links to state development banks; more emphasis on fixed assets in heavy industry; less tolerance for credit restrictions and high interest rates
Stabilization profile	Recurrent external bottlenecks lead to frequent periods of orthodox austerity backed by agro-exporters and large industrialists and opposed by popular sector groups	Access to external financing reduces pressure to undertake orthodox stabilization program; initiatives often opposed by business groups and abandoned when expansion is threatened; package of 1964-67 is only sustained program until 1980s

led or more market-oriented development strategies—a stalemate reflected in the sharp stop-go cycles depicted in Figures 2-A and 2-B. In Brazil, authorities confronted a much weaker popular sector and established more collaborative relations with international investment forces. Inflation thus had very different political and distributive implications. Whereas in Argentina it reflected and exacerbated an underlying sociopolitical stalemate, in Brazil it served for a number of decades as a mechanism for financing state-sponsored development projects and for transferring income to industrialists, professional groups, and other powerful interests (Baer and Kerstenetzky 1964). Until the early 1960s, when the economy finally began to encounter severe external bottlenecks, there was less pressure on state authorities in Brazil to attempt to stabilize prices or rein in expansionist economic policies. Orthodox initiatives were much more quickly abandoned in Brazil than in Argentina, growth rates were higher, and annual fluctuations in the rate of inflation were much less extreme (see Figures 2-A and 2-B).

I. Distributive Conflicts and International Constraints: Early Postwar Experiences

For an understanding of the distributive conflicts in Argentina and Brazil in the postwar period, the Perón and Vargas eras of the 1940s are essential points of departure. From 1943 to 1949, Perón's populism virtually transformed the political structure of Argentine society. Through state trading boards, the Peronists engineered a major redistribution of income from agrarian elites toward workers and small manufacturers. Government-backed unions extracted substantial wage concessions from the larger industrialists. Throughout the 1940s, the regime adopted a confrontational stance toward hegemonic interests in the international system—first by tilting toward the Axis powers, then by nationalizing U.S. and British packing houses and railroads. Brazil's experience under Vargas contrasted with Perón's form of radical populism on almost every point. Throughout the 1930s and 1940s, military elites, coffee exporters, industrialists, and rural bosses of the interior were the major components of Vargas's ruling coalition. Vargas began to bid for the support of workers in the mid-1940s, but he did so within the framework of extensive state-corporatist controls over union financing and leadership which placed heavy constraints on organized labor.

Figure 2-A

Fluctuations in GDP Rates in Argentina and Brazil, 1946–1960

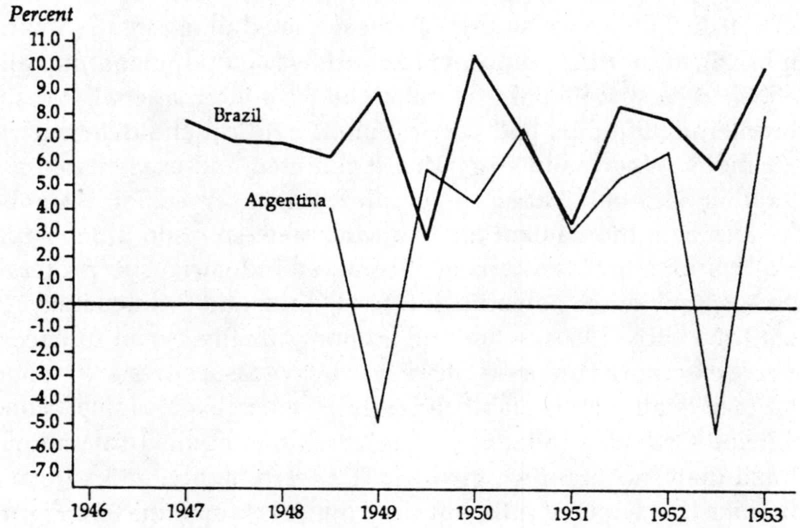

Figure 2-B

Fluctuations in Inflation Rates in Argentina and Brazil, 1946–1960

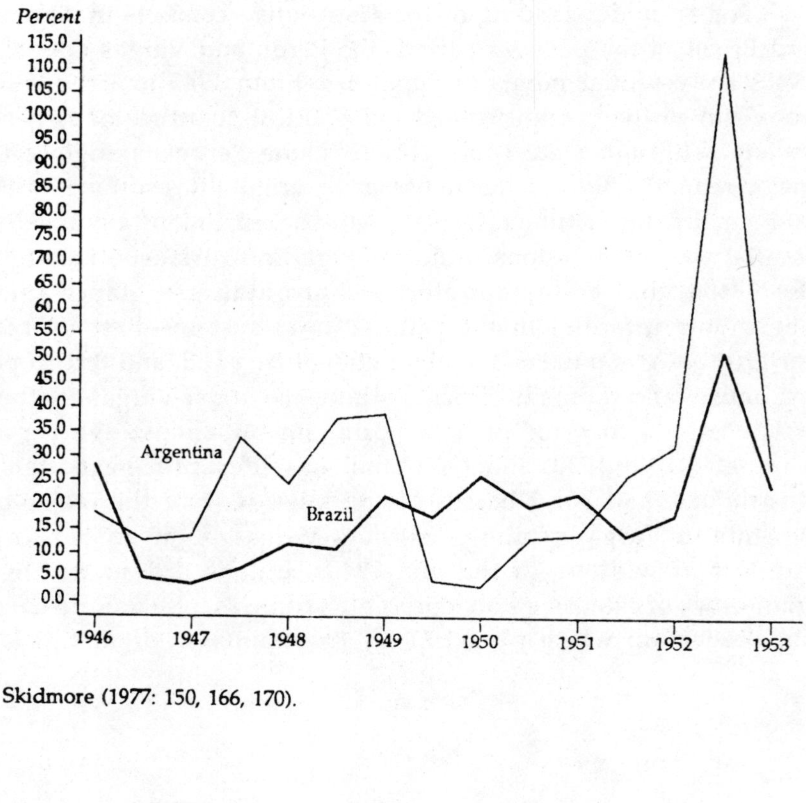

Source: Skidmore (1977: 150, 166, 170).

Finally, while Vargas also appealed to nationalist sentiments, he helped to lay the foundations of postwar economic goodwill by providing strong support for the Allied war effort: his was the only government in Latin America to send troops to the European front (Díaz-Alejandro 1978; Rock 1975; Ascher 1984; Wirth 1970; Skidmore 1967).

Virtually every Brazilian and Argentine government since World War II has operated in the shadow of these legacies (Skidmore 1979). Argentina entered the postwar world both isolated internationally and polarized domestically. Until the overthrow of Perón in 1955, Argentine governments remained unaffiliated with the Bretton Woods system and thus ineligible for World Bank funding or IMF loans. Whereas Brazil (and Mexico) began to receive major direct investment inflows around the mid-1950s, external investment did not become a major factor in the Argentine economy until the early 1960s—and only then in flows that fell off quickly during domestic political crises and economic downturns.

In the meantime, deep cross-cutting domestic cleavages impeded the consolidation of support for any of the development strategies being debated in the 1940s and 1950s. In their reactions against Perón's statist policies, the agrarian, financial, and industrial elites appeared more strongly attached than in Brazil to laissez-faire ideologies—despite the fact that much of the "upper bourgeoisie" had backed import-substitution policies in the 1930s. Throughout most of the 1950s and 1960s, however, the advocates of market-oriented policies were politically weak. In democratic contexts, they lacked numerical strength, and the Peronist-dominated union movement remained a powerful impediment to policies aimed at shifting resources from popular consumption into exports. In authoritarian contexts as well, liberal economic models typically ran into opposition not only from the popular sector but also from military nationalists and domestically oriented large industrialists, who tended to swing away from orthodox policies once balance-of-payments problems were brought under control.

Political cleavages in Argentina also made it difficult to mobilize sustained support for more "inward-oriented" approaches to development. In the late 1950s, for example, Arturo Frondizi's attempt to institute a version of Brazil's "developmentalist" model was fatally weakened by electoral rivalries between his Radical government and the Peronists, as well as by the suspicions of deeply anti-Peronist military officers and industrialists who might otherwise have provided support for his regime (Cavarozzi 1984; Wynia 1978).*

Brazil entered the postwar era less bitterly divided domestically than Argentina and better positioned to capitalize on various forms of external economic assistance. To be sure, as in Argentina, civil-military crises were ongoing components of the political process after 1945, accompanied by ideological controversy over the economic role of the state. In the early 1950s, for example, public ownership of the petroleum industry became a major point of contention between the Vargas government and its conservative critics. But unlike the dominant elites in Argentina, large-scale Brazilian industrialists and exporters had acquired strong vested interests in the subsidies and state investment policies established during the Vargas era,† and with unions extensively controlled by the state apparatus, they had less to fear from populist threats to redistribute income and power. Thus by the mid-1950s most segments of Brazil's big business elite had come to accept and profit from state-driven models of industrialization which, despite recurring problems with inflation, generated sufficient growth to reduce the intensity of struggles over resources (Skidmore 1967; Wirth 1970; Wallerstein 1980; Maxfield 1986).

Under what conditions were Argentine and Brazilian governments impelled to tackle inflationary problems? In both societies, domestic distributive conflicts eventually ran up against foreign exchange shortages which restricted the capacity to import capital equipment required to sustain economic expansion. At this point, authorities faced strong pressures to try to stabilize domestic prices in order to reduce speculation on foreign exchange, lower the demand for imports, and establish sufficient credibility among external creditors to increase the flow of foreign financial assistance.

This began to happen more and more frequently in both societies during the early and mid-1950s as the terms of trade began to decline

*A complementary explanation of the intensity of sectoral conflict in Argentina emphasizes that the principal exports (beef and wheat) have also been the main wage goods, which makes transfers of income between exporters and the domestic popular sector particularly transparent (O'Donnell 1977). It seems clear, however, that the political antagonisms described deepened and reinforced these cleavages emerging along economic lines.

†Hirschman has suggested that the role of coffee as an export staple encouraged Brazilian planters to seek state support because the long-term investment committed to initial cultivation of coffee trees inhibited short-term adjustment to price fluctuations (1981).

for beef and coffee. Figures 3-A and 3-B show the basic patterns of inflation and balance of trade in Argentina and Brazil during the 1950-1969 period. Regardless of their political base or ideological orientation, governments of all sorts began to turn in orthodox directions when they started to run out of money. During or immediately following sharp drops in reserve levels, Argentine governments of all kinds engaged in major stabilization initiatives, with two of the most orthodox and prolonged coming under Perón (1951–52) and the popularly elected Frondizi (December 1959–April 1961). The pattern is more complicated in Brazil, but there were repeated, short-lived initiatives under Vargas (October 1953–May 1954), Cafe Filho (August 1954–April 1955), Kubitschek (October 1958–June 1959), and Quadros (January–August 1961).

Though many factors influenced the design of these programs, their fiscal and monetary orthodoxy and duration appeared to be linked directly to the severity of the external accounts crisis and to the limits on access to foreign financing and investment. This placed early postwar Argentine governments at a disadvantage relative to Brazil and contributed substantially to the intense stop-go cycles Argentina experienced during those years. Since Argentine regimes generally had to cross higher "confidence thresholds" among external as well as domestic investors, it was harder than in Brazil to avoid programs emphasizing monetary and fiscal contractions, wage controls, and devaluations. The effectiveness of these measures in reducing inflation has been much disputed, even among conservative economists, but they did sooner or later relieve balance-of-payments pressures by reducing imports and/or attracting external financial assistance. By that time, however, incumbent governments (whether military or civilian) would find themselves in trouble politically, isolated from their own support bases, and under increasing pressure to return to more expansionist policies. At these points, either the incumbents or some new regime would typically relax the austerity program and begin the cycle again (Wynia 1977).

In Brazil, because of lower levels of domestic class conflict, it was easier to obtain external financing (see Table 2), which made it easier for governments to lengthen expansionary cycles and recover relatively quickly when balance-of-payments crises hit. Consequently, despite the repeated stabilization initiatives of the 1950s and early 1960s, there was less incentive than in Argentina for governments to follow through on orthodox fiscal or monetary commitments. In contrast to

Figure 3-A

Inflation Rate, International Reserves, and Balance of Trade in Argentina, 1950–1969

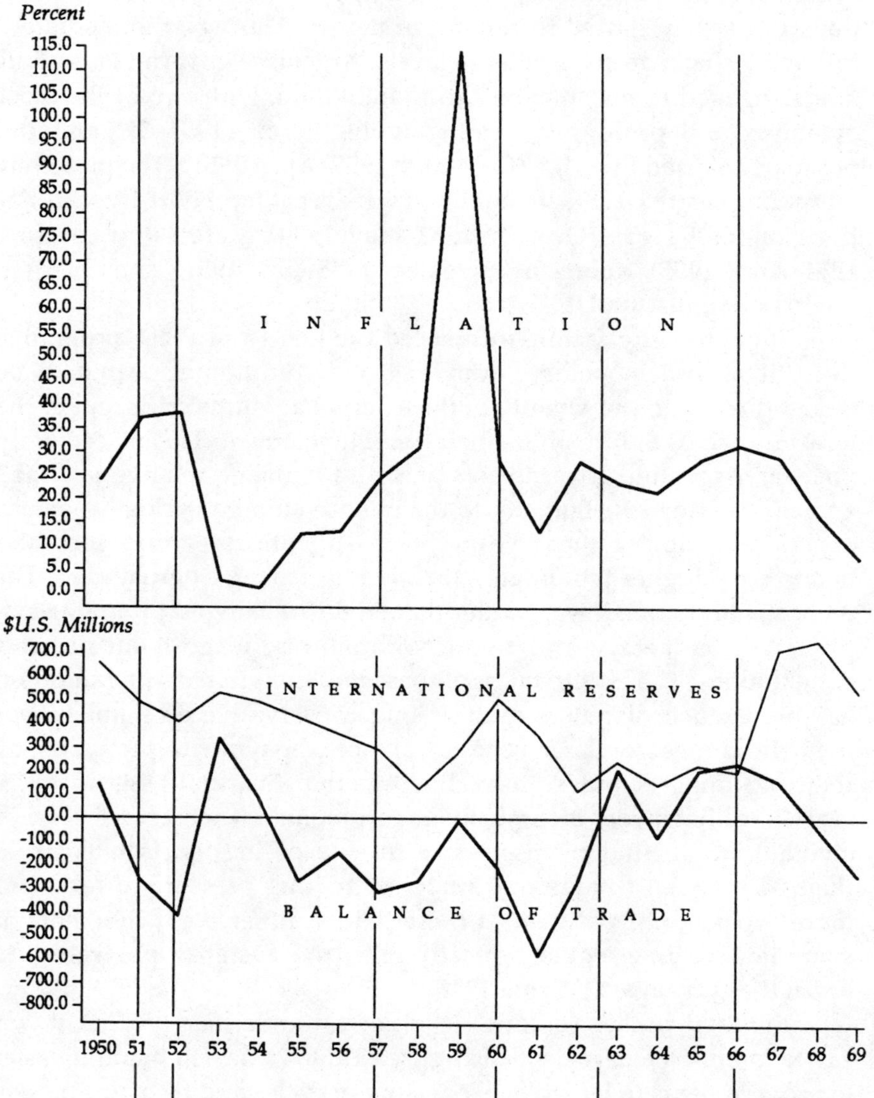

Sources: Inflation and balance of trade data—Skidmore (1977: 150, 163, 168); international reserves data—IFS.

Figure 3-B

Inflation Rate, International Reserves, and Balance of Trade in Brazil, 1950–1969

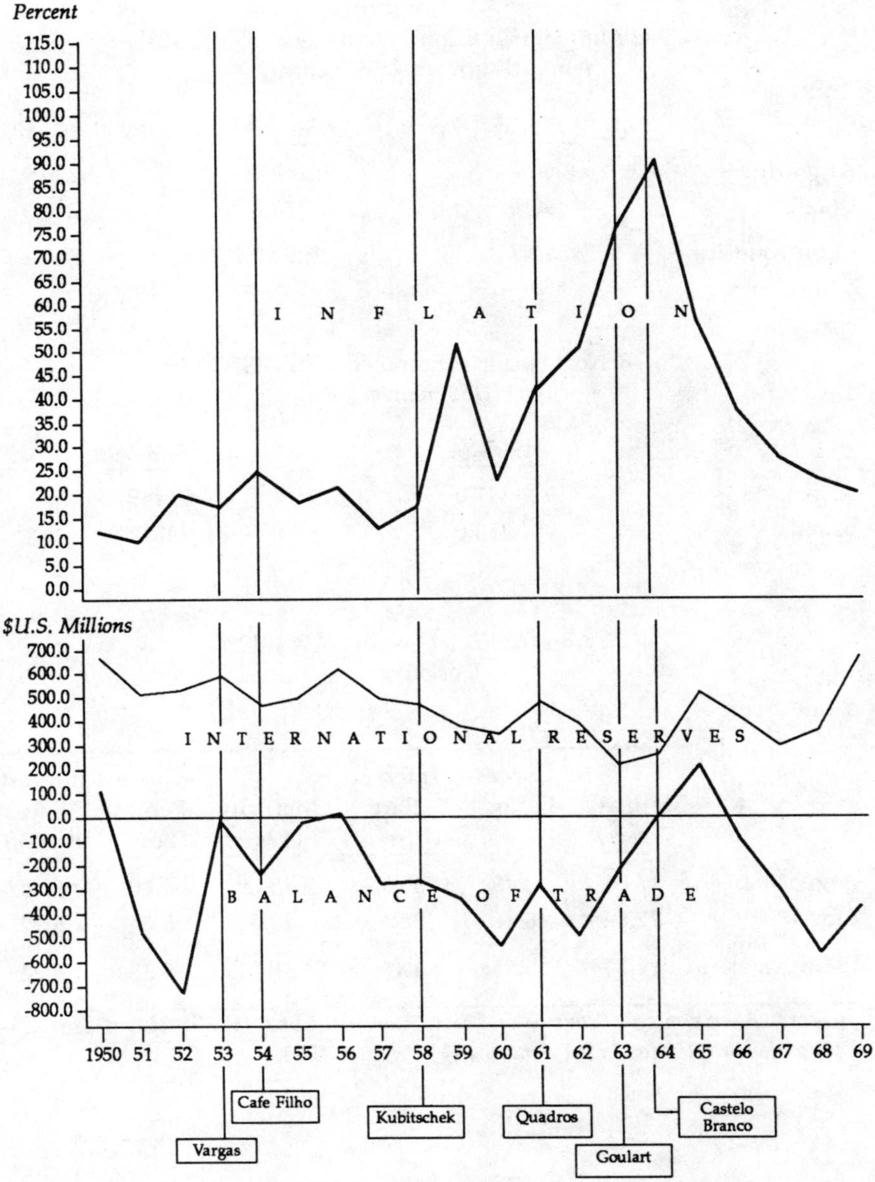

Sources: Inflation and balance of trade data—Skidmore (1977: 150, 163, 168); international reserves data—IFS.

Table 2

Types of External Capital Inflows in Latin America, 1951-1970

A. Net Autonomous Capital Movements, 1951–1963
(Annual averages, US$ millions)

	1951–55	1956–60	1961–63
Argentina	$ 60.7	$ 167.6	$220.9
Brazil	90.6	274.8	246.3
Latin America	511.7	1293.7	819.1

B. New Financial Resources, 1965–1970
(US$ millions)

	1965–67	1968–70
Argentina	$-347.0	$ 449.0
Brazil	250.0	2774.0

C. Terms of Official Lending, 1966–1970
(Averages)

	1966–67			1968–70		
	Maturity *(Years)*	Grace Period *(Years)*	Interest Rate *(Percent)*	Maturity *(Years)*	Grace Period *(Years)*	Interest Rate *(Percent)*
Argentina	17.06	3.79	4.45%	15.09	4.10	6.34%
Brazil	22.84	6.86	3.93	19.31	5.64	5.22
Latin America	19.70	5.54	4.16	18.91	5.38	5.22

Sources: A—*Economic Survey of Latin America, 1963* (1965: 44); B and C—*Economic Bulletin for Latin America* (17, 1: 106, 109).

the relatively sustained packages imposed under Perón and Frondizi (two years and seventeenth months respectively), none of the pre-1964 Brazilian programs lasted more than about eight months. In general, as Nathaniel Leff observes,"the political elite's commitment to economic development ended [such] programs as soon as they appeared seriously to restrict economic growth" (1968:101). All faced strong opposition not only from unions and popular sector groups, but also from Sao Paulo industrial elites and coffee planters, who on several occasions threatened to organize motorcades throughout the city of Sao Paulo to protest attempted cutbacks of coffee stockpiling.

The pivotal role which external financing played in the accommodation of such pressures reached a highpoint during the industrial boom of the Kubitschek years (1956–60). From about 1956 to 1958, the boom was fueled by a massive inflow of direct investment and long-term credits, which offset a sharp drop in the price of coffee. Then, as current accounts balances began to deteriorate in 1958–60, the government was able to turn to suppliers' credits and other forms of short-term private lending to avoid an IMF stabilization program and prolong the industrial expansion.

It was not until the early 1960s, when these additional sources of credit dried up, that the expansionary string at last began to run out. By 1964, after several years of stagflation and political conflict, a new authoritarian government imposed the first sustained stabilization program in Brazil's postwar history. Eventually, however, the developmentalist model pursued under Kubitschek came to serve as a prototype for expansionist policies pursued later under a military regime. As in the 1950s, the authoritarian governments of the 1970s used access to external credit to work around current accounts deficits and to avoid the kinds of orthodoxy recurrently imposed in Argentina.

As Guillermo O'Donnell (1977) has suggested, such patterns are more usefully understood as spirals than as cycles. In Argentina, each round of expansion/external crisis/stabilization had important cumulative impacts on the overall relations between state and society. Between the overthrow of Perón in 1955 and the military takeover of 1976, Argentina had experienced two minority Radical governments (1958–62 and 1963–66), two military regimes (1955–58 and 1966–73), a brief quasi-civil war (1962–63), and a return of the Peronists (1973–76). In a society deeply divided along political, class, and sectoral lines, each change of regime brought major shifts in personnel and policy. Each failure in turn weakened the authority of the state and left civil society more fragmented. Among industrial and agro-exporting elites, the lack of confidence compressed time horizons and reinforced tendencies to engage in short-term speculative activities. Within the Peronist movement, as well as the political parties generally, internecine conflicts intensified. After almost two decades of opposition, the Peronist party had evolved into a bitterly divided aggregate of social democrats, union bosses, fascists, and radical leftists—all linked by little more than personal attachment to Perón. Finally, in the late 1960s and early 1970s, the social crisis began to take on new dimensions as Peronist and Marxist terrorist groups threatened the personal security of military officers, business executives, and Peronist officials themselves.

In Brazil, less intense political divisions set a different long-term pattern into motion. The organization of the state's economic apparatus was much less caught up in the electoral rivalries of the 1940s and 1950s. Institutions such as the Bank of Brazil and Monetary Authority served as strongholds for technocratic personnel who were able to impart a substantial degree of continuity in economic policy. This bureaucratic stability, coupled with the expansionist approach pursued more or less consistently throughout the first postwar decades, helped to mute distributional conflicts among elites and to consolidate the ties between the state apparatus and key business interests. Organized workers also participated to some extent in the expansion of the 1950s, but their power to protect their interests was very limited. Despite some increase in real terms under Kubitschek, industrial wages in Brazil remained far below Argentine levels and comprised a smaller share of the national income. And despite their increased militancy during the administrations of Quadros and Goulart, the unions were too weak to prevent wages from being seriously eroded by accelerating inflation.

Thus when Brazil's elitist structure of power began to face serious economic and political challenges in the early 1960s, it rested on relatively secure institutional and political foundations. Recession, along with increasing union and peasant activity, contributed to perceptions that the system was in danger, but the threats faced by the Brazilian elites were far less severe than those which faced their Argentine counterparts a decade later. Despite the severity of the stagflation crisis, the Brazilian economy was not close to collapse, and until the very end of Goulart's presidency, powerful military and business interests were able to impose strict restraints on the government's support for popular movements and social reforms. Finally, although there was an upsurge of guerrilla activity during the late 1960s, Brazil never experienced the widespread breakdown of social controls and extensive terrorist violence that would later threaten the personal security of Argentina's ruling elites.

II. Bureaucratic-Authoritarian Regimes and the Transition to Democracy: The 1960s and 1970s

These cross-national differences had a profound impact on subsequent attempts by the Brazilian and Argentine military and technocratic elites to resolve the distributive conflicts in their societies by imposing authoritarian controls. There were, to be sure, important similarities between the Brazilian and Argentine authoritarianisms—particularly in their military-backed attempts to purge their political systems of populist influences*—but because each authoritarian regime confronted quite distinctive sets of challenges, they left different types of economic and political legacies for the constitutional governments succeeding them in the mid-1980s. In Brazil, the military government assumed control of a state apparatus that was more or less intact. While it increased the level of political repression at first, it felt sufficiently secure to allow room for political participation and dissent. After a period of tightened control from about 1968 to the early 1970s, the regime opened the way for the formation of an opposition movement and eventually for the transition to a civilian president in 1985. In contrast, the Videla government of Argentina conceived its mission in terms of a fundamental reconstruction of the relations between the state and civil society. It concentrated power in the hands of generals and neoclassical technocrats, engaged in bloody repression, and initiated a radical effort to open the economy to market forces.

The Economic Models. In Brazil the Castelo Branco military regime began its period in power (1964–67) with an important series of policy innovations, including tax and banking reforms and the first sustained package of monetary and fiscal austerity to be imposed in

*The 1966-70 period of military rule in Argentina under Organía is generally considered its first episode of bureaucratic-authoritarianism; although comparatively mild, it substantially deepened the political polarization (see O'Donnell 1973; Collier 1979). The focus here is on the second episode because it had greater impact and its legacy is more direct in the democratic period under consideration in this study.

the postwar era. However, these reforms both reflected and consolidated the power relations and economic policy approaches of the pre-1964 era (Fishlow 1973; Serra 1979; Evans 1979; Foxley 1983). Predictably the main costs of these policies were borne by workers, peasants, and small manufacturers—groups which had already lost ground during the inflationary upsurge of the early 1960s. In turn the upper strata of Brazilian society were the main beneficiaries of the developmentalist policies put into place toward the end of the decade. As in the 1950s, the key objective of these policies was to expand the heavy industrial base of the economy through extensive state credits, public investment, and the extension of subsidies and incentives to large domestic and foreign industrial investors.*

The parallels with the Kubitschek period were perhaps closest and most apparent in the period following the oil shocks of the 1970s. Despite a widening current accounts gap, both the Geisel (1974–79) and Figueiredo (1979–85) administrations—each committed to a relaxation of political controls—decided to avoid restrictive monetary and fiscal policies and push ahead with externally financed capital goods and infrastructural projects. As before, this allowed them to expand the industrial economy as well as deflect political opposition, but at the cost of a major buildup of external debt, annual inflation rates of about 50 percent, and eventually a severe decline in the creditor confidence required to sustain the process (Lamounier and Moura 1986).†

In 1981–83 access to external credit markets collapsed, and the regime entered a new period of crisis. For the second time since 1964 the administration was compelled to slam on the monetary brakes, inducing a sharp economic contraction. To reduce external accounts pressures, it also decreed major devaluations in 1979 and 1983 which helped to pave the way for experimentation with heterodox shock policies a few years later. In the interim, however, the orthodox stabilization program deepened the political and economic problems faced by the military regime. With the devaluations adding successive shocks to the indexed price system, inflation climbed to over 160 percent in 1983 despite extraordinarily severe monetary austerity. At the same time, a credit squeeze induced industrialists to step up their demands for

*An important new development was the promotion of industrial exports.

†The authors suggest that, as in the Kubitschek period, part of the motivation was to build popular support for the system during a period of political opening (170).

political reform (Frieden 1987), and a general recession—the worst since the 1930s—increased the pressure from the popular sector.

The post-1976 Argentine regime adopted a much more radical development strategy—and ended with a different type of economic crisis. The IMF-backed shock treatment pursued under Finance Minister Martinez de Hoz went far beyond Brazil's 1964–67 stabilization package in terms of monetary and fiscal austerity, and this in turn was closely linked to a long-term program based on sweeping deregulation of the capital market, banking system, and trade. Canitrot (1980: 913-28) has suggested that the underlying purpose of these measures was to implement a neoclassical cultural revolution aimed at forcing capitalists and workers into more "rational" forms of market-oriented behavior. Their effect by the mid-1980s was to sharply reduce and weaken the manufacturing sector (its share of the GDP declined from about 28 to 22 percent during the 1970s) and to concentrate economic power in the hands of a narrow financial-industrial elite specializing in speculative activities.

The most problematic aspect of the approach adopted under Martinez de Hoz was the decision to control inflation by allowing the peso to devalue at a slower rate than domestic prices. This was justified on the grounds that cheap imports would eventually stimulate increases in productivity, while high domestic interest rates would attract hard currency savings. By 1980–81, however, the strategy had begun to backfire badly. The overvalued peso had encouraged capital flight, placed severe pressures on external accounts, and put an end to the external financing that had fueled the brief consumer-goods import boom during the late 1970s. After massive state subsidies to the domestic financial sector failed to stem the tide, the regime was forced to assume direct responsibility for the huge private debt. In the meantime, to avert domestic attention from the collapsing house of cards, an increasingly isolated military government—unchecked by institutionalized structures of public accountability—launched the disastrous Malvinas/Falkland Islands adventure that led to its demoralization and collapse in 1983.*

Political Transitions and Distributive Politics. The changes of political regimes associated with these economic crises in Brazil and Argentina opened the way for the resurfacing of distributive political struggles centered in the party systems and the union movement.

*For critiques from various perspectives, see Felix (1983), Dornbusch (1984), Vasena and Szewach (1985), and Frenkel, Fanelli, and Winograd (1986).

Like the economic models, however, the national political transitions involved different degrees of incrementalism and discontinuity that would influence the way the new constitutional governments would deal with the distributive struggles (Viola and Mainwaring 1984; Mainwaring 1986; Smith 1986; Cavarozzi 1986a; Martins 1986). A brief discussion of the implications of these transitions is the final step before turning to direct analysis of the handling of the inflationary problems of the mid-1980s.

The shift to a constitutional government in Brazil, though pushed forward by substantial pressure from the anti-military opposition, completed a process of controlled liberalization initiated in the mid-1970s by the authoritarian Figueiredo regime itself. In 1984–85 the selection of a civilian president occurred within the framework of electoral college negotiations between moderate leaders of the PMDB (Brazilian Democratic Movement) opposition, headed by Tancredo Neves, and a breakaway faction of the pro-military party, headed by José Sarney. Sarney, who was initially the choice for vice-president, became head-of-state when Neves, the PMDB president-elect, died before he could take office. As with most earlier regime changes in Brazil, this type of incremental process ensured substantial continuity in the power of the military establishment and of the business and professional interests represented in the state bureaucracy.

At the same time, the political opening led to an upsurge in expectations and organized pressure for improvements in general standards of living. The PMDB—a huge catchall majority which dominated both the Congress and most state governorships—was itself an important source of pressure for federal funds and patronage. On the left, old-style radical populists—most prominently Lionel Brizola—also acquired substantial electoral strength during the mid-1980s. Perhaps most important, the constitutional opening enlarged opportunities for the expansion of a militant new workers' movement (headed by Luís Ignacio Lula da Silva—"Lula") which had begun to mobilize in a series of wildcat strikes in the metallurgical sector in the late 1970s. Though still weak at the national level, this movement was an important new force in the southern industrial heartland. By 1984 its political party had acquired a strong electoral presence in the state of Sao Paulo, and its peak union organization had become a powerful independent rival of the official General Confederation of Workers (CGT).

This combination of incremental transition from above and a surge of new distributive expectations from below resulted in difficult new choices for democratic officials seeking to deal with the economic crisis, as well as complex trade-offs for the system as a whole. The continuity of the underlying structure of power offered a more stable context for the recovery of private investment and the resurgence of an inherently dynamic industrial economy, but the optimism engendered by these prospects created high expectations for the electoral politicians after 1985. On the other hand, the continuing political influence of entrenched military and economic interests limited their freedom for distributing the burdens of stabilization and adjustment on an equitable basis.

In Argentina the transition to a constitutional regime occurred in the aftermath of the Malvinas Islands defeat in a sweeping, abrupt, and disorganized fashion. Faced with a massive wave of popular demonstrations and public protests, the military establishment was shattered and demoralized and acquiesced without conditions to direct presidential elections. A new caretaker Army government (the Navy and Airforce had withdrawn from the junta) was formed to supervise the process. To the surprise of most observers (and the participants themselves), the results of the elections exposed the weakness of the Peronists—the military's great adversary in the postwar period. Deeply divided, the Peronist party suffered its first electoral defeat in its history, and Alfonsín's hastily constituted Radical coalition was swept into office with the first genuinely free election victory since the 1920s.

As in Brazil, the change opened the way to a substantial escalation of distributive politics. Competition within and between the victorious Radicals and Peronists—each with strong traditions of patronage—provided one source of pressure. The unions, though weakened by past repression and high unemployment, also returned as a major force, and the dynamic young head of the CGT, Saul Ubaldini, who had risen to national prominence as a leader of mass demonstrations against the dictatorship, became a particularly important adversary of the Alfonsín government. Among the industrial federations, finally, old-line union bosses and militant "renovationists" competed for support among the rank and file.

What were the chances that the new government could deal with the economic crisis and the intensified distributive pressures within a constitutional framework? A major obstacle was the structural weakness and financial disarray of the Argentine economy. In some ways another abrupt regime transition compounded the problem by increasing the uncertainties of private investors, but although they were stretched very thin by the day-to-day tasks of political and economic reconstruction, the officials of the new Alfonsín administration did enjoy some advantages. One was that after the violence, military defeat, and economic roller-coaster of earlier decades, expectations were lower than in the past. Another was that the bureaucratic vacuum left by the hasty retreat of the military government gave the new decision-makers substantial freedom to frame new macroeconomic policies (but left them with a totally disorganized data-gathering apparatus). Finally, the weakening of the once-dominant military and Peronist veto groups offered opportunities to redefine broad relations between the state and key economic interest groups.

The full implications of these recent developments have yet to be played out in either Argentina or Brazil, but they appear to indicate two societies moving in very different directions with respect to class conflict and political representation. In Brazil there is movement toward an escalation of distributive conflicts over historic levels, while in Argentina movement is toward the possible emergence of a new political center. As we turn to a direct discussion of heterodox approaches in the two societies, we need to avoid a linear analysis which simply projects the past into the future. In the context of increasing class conflict and more restrictive international conditions, the elite-centered incrementalism that worked reasonably well for Brazil in past decades may not function so well in the future. Conversely, in Argentina, the weakening of old political antagonisms has created opportunities for organizing more economically viable mechanisms of democratic competition and legitimation.

The Austral and Cruzado Packages: 1985–1987

Escalating inflation became identified as an especially salient component of the contemporary economic crises in Argentina and Brazil from about 1983 onward—during the last months of military rule and approximately the first year of new constitutional government in each country. To be sure, there was also concern about other issues—most notably the huge debt obligations hanging over both societies—but by the mid-1980s the several years of deep recession had eased the current accounts squeeze and brought some relief from the pressures of external creditors. In the meantime, however, prices continued to soar upward. In Argentina, the consumer price index climbed from about 160 percent per year in 1982 to over 340 percent per year in 1983, as the outgoing military government sought to reduce social tensions by generous wage and credit policies. By the time of the Austral decree in June 1985, the monthly rate had doubled again to about 800 percent. In Brazil, hit by shocks from successive crop failures and devaluations, the inflation rate increased from about 50 percent to over 200 percent per year under Figueiredo. By the time of the Cruzado decree, monthly price increases were at a record high and were approaching an annual rate of 400 percent (see Table 3 and Figures 4-A and 4-B). Both Argentine and Brazilian officials were later criticized for focusing too narrowly on inflationary developments (or rather for ignoring their linkages to problems of debt servicing and structural adjustment), but it is not difficult to understand why concern about escalating prices came to occupy such a high place on their policy agendas.

The heterodox shock packages adopted as a response to these challenges resulted from a confluence of several different developments. One was the laying of the intellectual foundations of the programs by small groups of politically liberal economists seeking alternatives to the neo-orthodox programs being advocated by foreign creditors and many domestic neoclassical conservatives. A second factor was improvement in the external accounts situation, which expanded the space for experimentation with heterodox policies. A third factor was the transition to constitutional regimes, which opened the way for necessary changes in political orientation and key personnel. After a period of wavering between stimulative policies and economic orthodoxy, Alfonsín and Sarney both turned to new finance ministers—Juan Sourrouille in Argentina (appointed in February 1985) and Dilson Funaro in Brazil (appointed in August 1985)—who provided the critical political backing for the economists putting together the Austral and Cruzado packages.

Our next objective is to describe the evolution and implementation of these policies. First we look at the ideas of the economists and the interests of the politicians who directed the policy process. Then we review three phases of the process: the pre-decree period of debate within the bureaucracy, the post-decree honeymoon period, during which inflation dropped dramatically and the government's popularity surged, and the post-honeymoon period, when tough fiscal and monetary choices began to become necessary.

Table 3

Economic Performance in Argentina and Brazil, 1979-1986

Economic Index	Years							
	1979	1980	1981	1982	1983	1984	1985	1986
Gross Domestic Product [a]								
Brazil	6.4%	7.2%	-1.6%	0.9%	-3.2%	4.5%	8.3%	8.0%
Argentina	6.2	0.8	-6.2	-5.1	3.1	2.4	-4.4	5.5
Inflation [b]								
Brazil	55.4%	109.2%	113.0%	94.0%	164.9%	232.9%	223.3%	70.5%
Argentina	159.5	100.8	104.5	164.8	343.8	626.7	385.4	79.2
Balance of Trade [c]								
Brazil	$-2,840	$-3,823	$1,202	$ 780	$6,470	$13,090	$12,471	$10,500
Argentina	1,110	-2,519	-287	2,286	3,331	3,523	4,582	2,900
Median Wages								
Brazil				121.6	112.7	105.1	102.6	117.0
Argentina				80.1	100.5	127.1	107.8	109.4

Sources: Argentina: Dornbusch-de Pablo (1986); *Proceso,* 2 March 1987, p. 37; Brazil: Cardoso and Fishlow (1988); *Proceso,* 2 March 1987, p. 37.

[a] Percent rate of growth

[b] Brazil—1979-85: percent change in wholesale price index; 1986: percent change in consumer prices
Argentina—percent change in consumer prices

[c] Millions of current U.S. dollars

Figure 4-A

Monthly Inflation Rate in Consumer Prices: Argentina, January 1985–April 1987

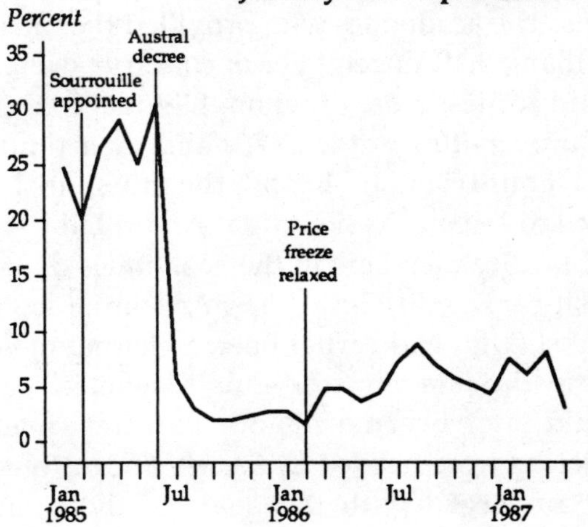

Figure 4-B

Monthly Inflation Rate in General Price Index: Brazil, January 1984–January 1987

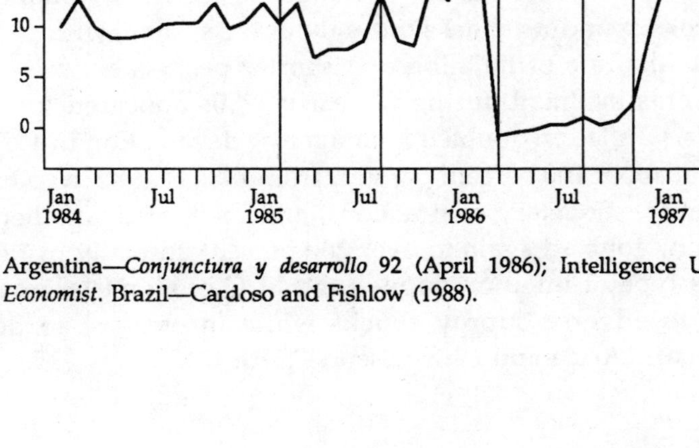

Sources: Argentina—*Conjunctura y desarrollo* 92 (April 1986); Intelligence Unit Report, *Economist*. Brazil—Cardoso and Fishlow (1988).

I. The Protagonists: Economists and Politicians

Throughout the decision-making process, policy initiatives were shaped most immediately by an alliance between academic economists and electoral politicians. The academics who provided the intellectual leadership —no more than a half dozen in each country—were young men in their thirties and forties, most of whom had received degrees from prestigious U.S. universities in the 1970s and then returned to careers in their own countries. In Brazil the most influential economists were Francisco Lopes, Persio Arida, André Lara-Resende, and Edmar Bacha—all faculty members in the economics department of the Catholic University at Rio (PUC-Rio). The Argentine economists included Roberto Frenkel (who had earlier been a visiting member of the PUC faculty), Mario Brodersohn, José Luis Machinea, and Juan Sourrouille, who would later become finance minister (Evans and Bruce 1986). The politicians were headed by Sarney and Alfonsín, and while their interests converged with the goals of the economists during the initial phases of the policy process, important differences began to emerge later on.

Not surprisingly the programs were conceived and designed by the economists. During the late 1970s they had been among many critics of orthodox "excess demand" explanations of inflation in their countries (e.g., Frenkel and O'Donnell 1979). By the mid-1980s the economics department at PUC-Rio had become a center for the elaboration of an alternative set of "inertial" explanations, which provided the basis of the new policies (Lara-Resende 1984; Arida and Lara-Resende 1985; Lopes 1984, 1986). The alternative analysis rested on two central points: first, in an "indexed society," inflation in any given contract period would always be reproduced in the following one; second, price shocks in any sector of the economy would quickly produce corresponding shocks throughout the system, with an overall increase in the rate of inflation and shorter periods between adjustments. Events in Brazil during the early 1980s appeared to validate this analysis. Inflation doubled after a major devaluation in 1979, then persisted at about 100 percent per year from 1980 to 1982 in spite of unusually severe monetary contractions, and then, after another major devaluation, doubled again to over 200 percent annually in 1984 and 1985. This type of inflation, argued the PUC economists, was "very sensitive to adverse supply shocks while insensitive to demand management" (Arida and Lara-Resende 1985: 43).

This analysis provided no clear-cut solution to the problems of inflation—a point readily acknowledged by the economists themselves—but it indicated a need to supplement conventional fiscal and monetary restraints with administrative steps to "de-index" the economy and break the inertial cycles (*ibid.*, 31). The principal instruments to be used were a wage/price freeze and a phased conversion of the old currency into a new one at successively devalued rates of exchange. The advocates of these measures warned that allocative distortions might result from freezing prices at very different points in their respective adjustment cycles. But they argued that these risks could be reduced by pre-decree adjustment of public tariffs and wages and realignment of prices through currency conversion tables. In any event, with prices galloping toward hyperinflation, the risks of their new policies were not likely to be as great as continued reliance on orthodox fiscal and monetary shock treatments.

Several factors eased the way for broader acceptance of these ideas. First, critiques of IMF-style demand-containment approaches were already widespread in both societies—not only among economic structuralists, but also among more orthodox economists as well. Second, the heterodox economists themselves benefitted from the prestige derived from training in the United States and international contacts. By the mid-1980s their inertial inflation arguments began to attract increasing attention among leading U.S. economists (see, e.g., Williamson 1985), which helped to legitimate their views at home.

Despite their impressive academic credentials, however, the heterodox economists were until 1985 quite marginal to the political process, with no substantial links to the newly ascendant Radical and PMDB parties and no connections to organized economic interests. The translation of their ideas into policy thus depended entirely on the sponsorship of the political elites.

For the heads of state, policies of inflation-control had to be balanced against other power considerations. Each president had prior commitments to key allies within his governing coalition and a need to maintain broad support within the electorate. Moreover, the strategy of sudden de-indexation proposed by the heterodox economists involved major political and economic risks in societies where adjustments for inflation had become embedded in the routines of daily life. In the initial phases of their administrations, such considerations led Alfonsín and Sarney to try other approaches first. In Argentina, the first finance minister was Alfonsín's Radical comrade-in-arms Bernardo Grinspun, who followed an expansionist and nationalist policy that brought him into increasingly acrimonious confrontations with the IMF and other international creditors. For the first six months of Sarney's administration, the cabinet he had inherited from Tancredo Neves remained divided by conflicts between "developmentalist" Planning Minister Joao Sayad* and finance minister Francisco Dornelles, a neoclassical economist advocating an IMF-backed stabilization package. The turning points in both societies came with the appointments of new finance ministers—Sourrouille in Argentina and Funaro in Brazil—which began the bureaucratic processes leading to the new stabilization decrees.

What impelled this change of direction? By the end of 1984 the political and economic situation in Argentina had become particularly desperate. After almost a year of tense confrontations with its creditors, debt-restructuring negotiations had reached an impasse, and the Alfonsín government was reluctantly moving toward acceptance of an IMF-style package. During the last quarter of the year, real interest rates rose sharply, and the economy had entered a severe recession, while inflation continued to spiral upward. By the time Sourrouille became finance minister in early 1985, the economy appeared near collapse. In Brazil, which was beginning a recovery from a 1981–83 depression (see Table 3), the pressure to change policy was far less severe. Nevertheless, there was widespread concern about the 200 percent annual inflation rate that had persisted through 1984 and 1985. When Funaro was appointed finance minister in August 1985, the monthly rate of increase had reached what was then an all-time high. In the meantime Sarney had come under increasingly sharp attack for his inability to take charge of his divided cabinet. His decision to oust the relatively orthodox Dornelles was his initial response to such criticisms, and his choice of Funaro, a Sao Paulo industrialist, signalled a commitment to a more explicitly developmentalist approach.

Within the context of these ministerial changes, the proposals by the heterodox economists served several important political purposes. First, despite their challenge to neoclassical stabilization arguments, they offered an important "centrist" alternative to the riskier proposals for debt-repudiation, state control, and radical income redistribution espoused by sectors of the left, the Peronists, and the

*Sayad, as planning minister, along with academic collaborators centered in Sao Paulo, initiated the contacts with the PUC economists that eventually led to the Cruzado (see Solnik et al. 1987).

Brazilian union movement. Indeed, the consolidation of heterodox shock programs presupposed favorable investment responses on the part of the Brazilian and Argentine private sectors. At the same time, because the proposals focused intensively on anti-inflation objectives, they postponed the need to choose right away between long-term state-directed and market-oriented strategies of adjustment. Earlier demand-management packages often suffered politically from the fact that they were identified with interests espousing economic liberalism. The heterodox shock proposals, in contrast, could attract support from groups backing very different kinds of long-term economic models.

Most important, the proposals were framed explicitly as "nonrecessive" approaches to stabilization, which avoided the short-term contractions associated with conventional demand-management approaches. This was an obvious boon for popularly based political elites. By the beginning of 1985, this was clearly a benefit for Alfonsín, then confronting a deepening economic depression, and in Brazil it offered some hope that inflation could be reduced without slowing high rates of growth. Later on, substantial tensions were to develop between the economists and the political leaders over the issue of electoral populism, especially in Brazil, but in the initial stages of the decision-making process, the technical recommendations of the economists seemed tailor-made to the support-building needs of the politicians.

II. The Pre-Decree Period: From New Finance Ministers to Initial Shocks

After the appointments of the new finance ministers, the initial stabilization decrees were shaped during several months of intra-bureaucratic bargaining and secretive planning among a small circle of economists and top-level executives—in order, it was later explained, to preclude economic interests from scrambling for advantage from an anticipated price freeze. Within this context, the two factors that seemed most crucial in shaping the programs were (1) the autonomy of the decision-making group within the state apparatus and (2) the degree of leverage the group could wield vis-à-vis the IMF, other external creditor groups, and allied domestic business elites. Because the Sourrouille group had greater autonomy within the domestic bureaucracy than the Brazilian group did, it had greater opportunities for pre-decree planning. More limited leverage vis-à-vis creditors, on the other hand, contributed to a priority for fiscal and monetary controls.

The bureaucratic autonomy of the Sourrouille group derived both from the intensity of the economic crisis and the character of the political transition in Argentina. In February 1985, there was no other politically acceptable group around Alfonsín with coherent ideas for dealing with recession and galloping inflation. Once he had turned to Sourrouille, the president could back his choice with formidable political resources. As Argentina's first elected president in ten years, and the only Radical ever to defeat a Peronist candidate, Alfonsín occupied a commanding position within both the Radical party and the constitutional system as a whole, despite mounting dissatisfaction with the economic situation. With Alfonsín's political support, Sourrouille was able to dominate cabinet-level deliberations.

On the other hand, while the Argentine elite enjoyed substantial leeway in dealing with domestic political and bureaucratic interests, its external room for maneuver was quite limited. A sharp drop in imports during the 1980-83 recession had produced some improvement in the balance of trade, but Argentina faced far greater external constraints than Brazil, where a surge of export revenues following devaluations in 1979 and 1983 had contributed to enormous surpluses (see Figures 5-A and 5-B). In addition, Finance Minister Grinspun's acrimonious exchanges with the IMF during 1984 had backed Argentina into a corner—more than $1.6 billion in arrears on external interest payments, facing a suspension of previously negotiated U.S. treasury and bank loans, and a refusal by Paris Club authorities to step into the breach (Bouzas and Keifman 1985: 113-19). Finally, there was a need to coax investment capital out of a very insecure financial-industrial elite which had already diverted a large share of its assets abroad. Toward the end of 1984, the premium paid for dollars on the black market—often taken as a barometer of financial confidence—shot up to almost 75 percent after having fallen to around 20 percent earlier in the year. Such factors led the Sourrouille team to place high priority on making its anti-inflation measures credible to both domestic and international business sectors, which included gaining the endorsement of the IMF.

The design of the Austral package bore the imprint of these domestic opportunities and external constraints. On the one hand, by appealing to the U.S. Treasury and Federal Reserve for assistance, the

Figure 5-A

Exports and Imports in Argentina, 1979–1986

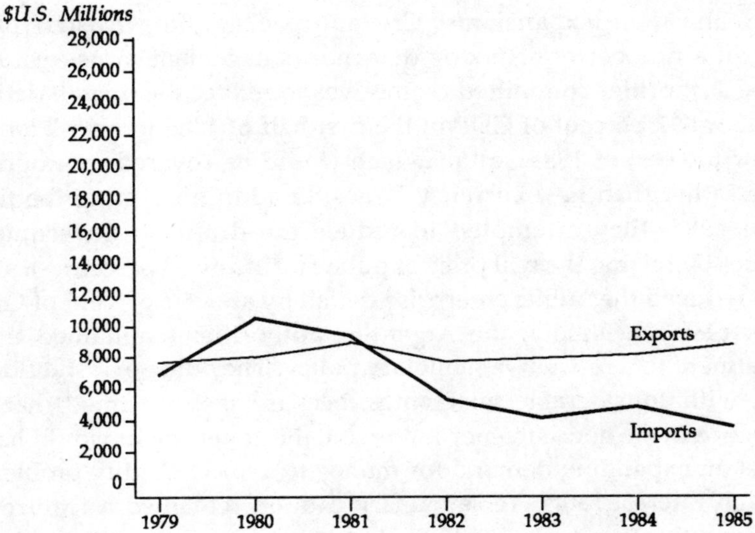

Figure 5-B

Exports and Imports in Brazil, 1979–1986

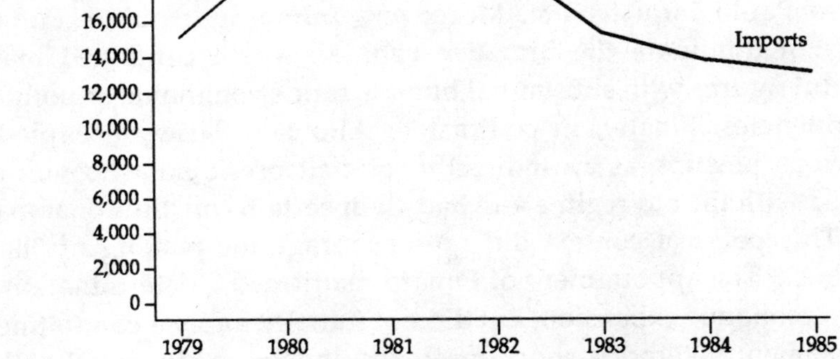

Sources: Brazil—Cardoso and Fishlow (1987); Argentina—Dornbusch and De Pablo (1987).

Alfonsín government was able to obtain IMF approval of the price freezes and currency reforms, signalled by the announcement of a new IMF agreement just a few days before the Austral decree. Yet in contrast to the more expansionist Cruzado package, the Austral plan relied on a number of orthodox demand-management measures. Argentine authorities committed themselves to reduce the overall deficit from about 12 percent of GDP in the first half of 1985 to only 2.5 percent for the rest of 1985—all of which would be covered by external credits rather than new currency issues. In addition, during the first half of 1985, they attempted to reduce the drain on government revenues by raising the real price of public tariffs by 33 percent—a step which reduced the public enterprise deficit by about 2 percent of GDP (Lopes 1985:12). Finally, the Argentine authorities maintained their commitment to a restrictive monetary policy. They did so, it should be noted, with considerable misgivings, because they assumed that as confidence in the new currency increased, the government would have to meet an expanding demand for money to avoid liquidity problems and high interest rates. Yet monetary caution remained a feature of government policy during 1985-86 despite real interest rates reaching annual levels up to 60 percent during the first eight months of the Austral program (*El Bimestre* 27, 3 [1986]: 15-18).

The apparent success of the Argentine experiment in bringing down inflation during the second half of 1985 helped to smooth the way for the emergence of a similar plan in Brazil eight months later. However, the Brazilian version was framed within a very different matrix of bureaucratic politics and external constraints. On the one hand, the negotiated character of the political transition in Brazil placed severe limits on the leverage of the PUC economists within the decision-making apparatus. Unlike the Sourrouille group, the Rio-based Brazilian academics did not initially have close ties to Funaro, the Sao Paulo industrialist. Moreover, unlike Sourrouille, Funaro could not dominate the Brazilian cabinet, which contained many powerful figures with substantial bureaucratic strongholds or political constituencies. Finally, in contrast to Alfonsín, Sarney occupied a precarious position as an indirectly selected president who was associated with the old regime and had an uncertain constitutional mandate. This political context did not encourage the making of "hard decisions." The appointment of Funaro reaffirmed a determination to sustain economic expansion, but did not initially imply a commitment to implement heterodox shock measures. Indeed the impression that the Argentine Austral program had been recessionary helped delay a final presidential decision on the Cruzado package until almost the last minute.

On the other hand, Brazil enjoyed far greater room for maneuver with respect to external creditors and domestic investors than did Argentina. From 1984 through the first half of 1986, Brazil's monthly trade surplus had been averaging about $1 billion—one of the highest in the world. This gave Funaro the option of hardening Brazil's bargaining stance toward the international financial establishment. Whereas Sourrouille was impelled to seek IMF approval for his stabilization package, Funaro quickly broke off negotiations with the Fund and declared his intent to frame domestic policy and bargain with private banks without the Fund's supervision. The surge of export-led growth in 1984-85 encouraged the impression that, despite continuing difficulties with inflation, the economy had experienced a major adjustment in 1981-83. The hope was that a sudden price/currency reform would break the inertial cycle and help clear the way for a new wave of investment and expansion.

In early 1986 a final decision on the Cruzado program was forced by a sharp escalation of monthly inflation rates combined with mounting PMDB criticism of immobilism within the administration. The new decree differed in several important ways from its Argentine predecessor. First of all, fiscal policy was based on the assumption that operational deficits (i.e., the deficits corrected for the obligations incurred through an indexed public debt) had been substantially reduced by the austerity of 1981-83 and by changes in the tax laws instituted in December 1985. Thus there was reason to believe that "after the end of the temporary freeze, zero inflation would persist" without spending reductions or tax increases (Arida and Lara-Resende 1985: 31). Second, unlike in Argentina, public prices were frozen at relatively low real levels—along with key consumer products in the private sector, such as automobiles and meat. Third, monetary policy was much more expansionist. To avoid what was perceived as an unnecessarily recessive policy in Argentina, the M1 supply was doubled over the first three months of the program. Real interest rates, which had turned negative after Funaro's appointment, dropped further during the first quarter of 1986 (Cardoso and Fishlow 1988). Finally, in contrast to the Austral's cautious approach to wages, the Cruzado decreed a 33 percent increase in the minimum wage plus an across-the-board bonus of 8 percent—strongly stimulative measures in a context where real wages had already been rising for six months. As an insurance measure (urged by Labor Minister Pazzianotto, an ex-union lawyer), an automatic wage increase was guaranteed at any time the inflation rate surpassed 20 percent. The activation of this "wage trigger" became an important factor in the subsequent unravelling of the plan (Faria 1986: 29).

III. Implementation: The Honeymoon Phase

The months immediately following the announcements of the decrees marked the highpoints of the alliances between economists and politicians. As the economists had forecast, the decrees broke the inertial cycles: within only a month or two, inflation rates had dropped to close to zero in both Argentina and Brazil. The price freezes were immensely popular in both societies, and were initially reinforced by voluntary self-restraint and consumer monitoring. In Argentina the entire price control system was administered by a staff of about thirty. In the weeks following the Brazilian decree, thousands of citizens responded to appeals to act as "Sarney's auditors" by reporting price violations to the authorities.

Even more important, these objectives had been accomplished without prolonged contractions—indeed in both cases with substantial reactivation of the economies based in part on a strengthening of popular-sector incomes. In Argentina, the recession which had begun in late 1984 deepened somewhat in the months immediately following the Austral decree, but the situation had turned around by the end of 1985 (see Table 4), with strengthened demand for food and services contributing to the upswing. During 1986, the economy expanded at a brisk 5.5 percent. The Brazilian economy, which was already in high gear at the time of the Cruzado decree, accelerated still more—spurred by the big wage increases that had accompanied the package. Between March 1985 and March 1986, consumption increased by an incredible 30 percent. The industrial sector, still with excess capacity left over from 1981-83, grew at a rate of about 12 percent during this period (*Conjunctura Economica*, 15 July 1986, p. 9). Eventually the overheating of the economies became an issue of major concern, but the initial phases of the programs in both countries provided plenty of ground for optimism—especially when one considers the costs so often associated with more orthodox alternatives.

For the political leaders, the payoff for the next six months or so

Table 4

Economic Performance in Argentina, 1983-1986

	Median Wages		GDP	
	CEPAL[a] (1983=100)	INDEC[b] (1983=100)	FF/Econ[c]	DD[d]
1983				
I	81.4	93.3		
II	90.7	94.2		
III	99.7	104.5		
IV	107.9	107.9		
1984				
I	116.1	126.7	1.5%	
II	120.1	123.3	1.1	
III	117.9	122.4	0.2	
IV	125.9	128.3	-0.4	
1985				
I	115.4	121.6	-2.3	
II	106.4	106.0	-2.1	-2.9%
III	94.5	115.6	-3.4	
IV	101.2	118.2	4.7	-6.8
1986				
I			0.8	0.4
II			6.1	5.7
III			11.7	11.8
IV			4.7	

Sources: Sevares (1986:6); Frenkel and Fanelli (1986); *Economist;* (1987: 11); Dornbusch and De Pablo (1987).

[a]Comisión Económica para América Latina: deflation by inflation rate of preceding month.

[b]Instituto Nacional Estadística y Censos; deflated by inflation rate in month of payment.

[c]Frenkel and Fanelli/*Economist*.

[d]Dornbusch and De Pablo; 1985 semester figures based on percent change over same period preceding year.

was a huge surge of grass-roots support. In Argentina, popular approval ratings of the administration increased from 35 to 57 percent after mid-1985, while Alfonsín's already high personal popularity rose from 64 to 74 percent (per Encuesto Socmerc). In Brazil, Sarney's personal approval rating (favorable minus unfavorable) turned around from a negative 36 percent in January 1986 to a positive 68 percent in March, while confidence in the government as a whole increased from 40 percent in September 1985 to 72 percent in September 1986 (*Veja:* 17 December 86, 14 January 87).

Such support, it should be noted, rested almost entirely on direct appeals from the administrations to the populations at large. The decrees had been drafted without consultation outside the bureaucratic apparatus, and they were promulgated without congressional approval, without discussions with business leaders, and over the opposition of the heads of the major unions. This left a number of unresolved (or exacerbated?) problems to be faced with respect to policy adjustments and the larger issue of constitutional consolidation. But although some political opponents of the regime voiced strong initial criticisms of the stabilization initiatives, struggles among organized interests did not become visible until months later. Attempts by union leaders to organize protest strikes against the decrees fizzled out or were abandoned, while other critics on the left and right were drowned out by a chorus of approving comment from the press, business leaders, and their own associates. In congressional and gubernatorial elections held several months after each decree (November 1985 and November 1986 respectively), the Argentine Radicals and the Brazilian PMDB won landslide victories which appeared to place them in commanding positions politically.

IV. Implementation: The Post-Honeymoon Phase

Economic problems had begun to appear, however, well before these electoral triumphs. From the outset of each program, it was evident that decision-makers would eventually have to deal with questions about how to exit from systems of administered prices, as well as with even larger issues of economic restructuring, but the problems requiring most immediate attention were signs of overheating, shortages, and resurgent inflation that began to appear after the first several months of the price freeze. By about the second or third quarter of 1986, the situation in each country looked something like this:

INFLATION

Argentina: Authorities decided to adjust prices upward in April 1986. Monthly inflation rates, which had averaged about 1–3 percent during earlier months climbed to 7–9 percent by July and August 1986. Although this was far better than the 30 percent rates of the pre-Austral period, it raised significant concern about a new escalation of prices.

Brazil: Although the official price index showed close to zero rate of inflation, shortages and illegal surcharges had become widespread by mid-1986, with long queues to buy automobiles and other consumer durables and considerable speculation in meat and dairy products.

FISCAL AND MONETARY PERFORMANCE

Argentina: By early 1986, although interest rates continued at very high levels, the Argentine money supply was expanding somewhat faster than authorities desired as a result of the Central Bank's unmonitored rediscount loans to overextended provincial banks. Fiscal objectives were maintained for most of this period as a result of gains in the real value of tax revenues, but new taxes and/or major expenditure cuts would be required to sustain this balance.

Brazil: Authorities began to tighten monetary restrictions and raise interest rates to positive levels by the second quarter of 1986. However, fiscal deficits, strained by external debt payments, social services, and political patronage, remained a major problem. Originally projected at only 1 percent of GDP, the deficit was recalculated at about 5 percent by the middle of 1986.

EXTERNAL ACCOUNTS

Argentina: With its economy expanding, Argentina had begun to experience significant strain on trade balances. By mid-1986 it was clear that it would not meet a hoped-for surplus in the 3–4 billion dollar range (actual 1986 surplus was about 2.9 billion), and there was mounting pressure on the dollar/austral exchange rate.

Brazil: Began to experience a noticeable fall-off in monthly trade surplus by the third quarter of 1986. In September the balance fell to $840 million; by October and November it had fallen to $210 and $131 million.

The deepening trade-offs between expansionist objectives and control of inflation increased the strains on the alliance forged between the politicians and their economic advisors, marking the end of the honeymoon period. During 1986, advisors in both countries began to press for tighter monetary and/or fiscal controls. However, choices made primarily at the political level produced contrasting courses of action in the two countries. The Sarney administration continued in an essentially expansionist direction which by early 1987 had led to a collapse of the Cruzado program. The Alfonsín government took more substantial steps to manage the imbalances, and although long-term results remained unclear, the inflation was at least temporarily kept under control.

BRAZIL. In Brazil, emerging problems of excess demand had become evident to economists inside and outside the Sarney administration by the end of the first half of 1986. As early as April and May, advisors such as Arida and Lara-Resende had begun to press strongly within the administration for an adjustment in price levels and a tightening of fiscal and monetary controls (Solnik et al. 1987). In July, moderately orthodox economists associated with the prestigious Getulio Vargas Institute had begun to express concern publicly on the editorial pages of *Conjunctura Econômica*, warning that "without an appropriate correction" in fiscal and price policy, "inflation would return, along with the need to apply still more restrictive measures" (15 July 86). Business leaders, although publicly praising the plan, also argued vigorously in private for adjustments in the freeze on relative prices.

An important turning point came at a high-level conclave held at the end of May in the town of Carajas. In several days of discussions with the president, Funaro, Sayad, and other key ministers, the original architects of the program argued vigorously that substantial changes in taxes, public tariffs, and credit policy would be required to reduce some of the consumer demand driving the economy. Although it was clear that the initial package had been too expansionist, it did not appear too late to ease down on the fiscal or monetary brakes, or to relieve some of the allocative pressures that had been accumulating under the price freeze (Solnik et al. 1987).* However, with crucial congressional elections approaching in November, Sarney and Funaro decided against any major changes at this point in a policy course with

*There were, however, important divisions over how this should be accomplished. Arida and Lara-Resende, arguing that there had been a long-term shift in demand, pressed for deep cutbacks in fiscal spending and tighter monetary policy. Sayad, as head of the "spending ministry," pressed for increased taxes as a means of covering fiscal shortfalls.

such wide popularity. Sarney felt that a large PMDB victory was essential to his influence, since the new Congress would also serve as a constituent assembly that would decide the length of the presidential term. As long as they could bask in the glow of the Cruzado, PMDB congressional and gubernatorial candidates were not about to dissent from his position.

For most of the second half of 1986, therefore, the government's response to warnings about excess demand was a largely ineffective patchwork of measures. In July the administration decreed "compulsory savings" fees on various middle-class consumption items, including air fares, gasoline, and automobiles, but these were far more limited than the key economists within the Treasury and the Central Bank had hoped for. To preserve the illusion of zero inflation, the government ruled that the fees should be excluded from the price index, which evoked a bitter protest from Edmar Bacha, one of the PUC economists and then the head of the government's statistics agency. The new package—the Cruzadinho—angered middle class consumers, but it had limited effect on either the fiscal deficit or the consumption boom. Follow-up efforts over the next several months were concentrated primarily on highly publicized, but equally ineffectual, "supply-side" attempts to relieve food shortages, such as arranging for large-scale imports or, at one point, sending government trucks to try to find herds of cattle reportedly being hoarded in the interior.

In late November, a few weeks after the congressional elections, the government decreed a new "surprise package" (again without warning or consultation) that at last attempted a more decisive tightening of fiscal and monetary controls. Cruzado II provided for major increases in public tariffs on postage, electricity, fuel, water, and telephones, and new excise taxes on cigarettes and beer. It announced the closing or merger of fifteen state companies. It allowed interest rates on treasury bonds to float upward (nominal 60-day rates had hit 300 percent by January), and it reintroduced a system of mini-devaluations for the currency. In a move evoking bitter opposition from the labor unions, the government attempted to circumvent the wage-trigger provisions of the original Cruzado program by creating a new inflation index, showing lower price rises, and limiting the coverage of the adjustment provisions. Finally, although it attempted to maintain the general price freeze, it provided for selective increases in a number of private sector prices, including an 80 percent rise in automobile prices (Cardoso 1987).

By this time, opportunities for effective policy adjustments along these lines had been narrowed substantially by the buildup of speculative pressures and the decline of current accounts surpluses. Nevertheless, the rapid unravelling of the government's package over the next several months owed at least as much to the fire storm of political protest as to economic constraints. Charges of betrayal over the sudden attempt to change course came from virtually every corner of the political system. In late November, a CUT protest march in Brasilia directed against the new wage index ended in violence, with the police using tear gas and mobs setting fire to automobiles and banks. For the first time, the CGT began to collaborate with the CUT in plans to organize a general strike for the following month. Meanwhile, PMDB notables, fresh from their landslide victories, now began to express outrage that they had not been consulted about the government's shift in direction and to insist that some of the harsher provisions of Cruzado II be softened. Sarney's popularity ratings plummeted.*

In December, with the government relenting in part on its wage policy, the 20 percent adjustment trigger began to go off. In January and February, industrialists began to threaten that they would no longer obey government price control regulations (*Veja*, 21 January 87). Under these pressures the administration ended the freeze, and the dam burst. By the end of February, monthly price rises had escalated to pre-Cruzado levels, the huge trade surpluses had totally disappeared, and the government announced that it would suspend interest payments on its external commercial debt until a new debt rescheduling package could be arranged with creditors. By this time, policy disagreements had led to the resignation one by one of all of the original architects of the Cruzado policy, eventually including Funaro himself. Because Brazil still had a very strong underlying economy, and most political actors were committed to move forward with the constitutional transition, these developments did not entail political or economic collapse, but they did mark a disappointing end to a policymaking chapter that had begun with great optimism.

ARGENTINA. The Alfonsín government failed to restore full price stability to the Argentine economy, but from 1985 through 1987 incremental adjustments in the original Austral package allowed the government to maintain significantly lower rates of inflation than in

*Sarney's personal approval ratings, which had gone from negative 36 percent in January 1986 to positive 68 percent in March, plunged again to negative 22 percent by December 1986 (*Veja*, 14 January 87, p. 29).

the pre-Austral period. A new phase of the Argentine program opened in March 1986, when the government began to adjust prices upward and ended the freeze on the Austral/dollar exchange rate. This helped to reduce the hoarding and illegal surcharges that began to characterize the Brazilian economy at about the same time, but it also raised the specter of a resumption of the inflationary spiral. The Sourrouille group responded to this challenge with increased attempts to tighten monetary controls and contain wage demands. For the next twelve months or so, these efforts yielded some noteworthy gains on several fronts.

One of the most important of these was negotiating wage adjustments with the Peronist-dominated unions. The Alfonsín administration had gotten off to a terrible start with these groups in early 1984 by attempting to pass union reform legislation that offended most major factions of the Peronist movement. Wage strikes and general strikes, led by CGT head Saul Ubaldini, had surged during the early years of Alfonsín's term, subsided after the announcement of the Austral decree, but then began to surge again by the end of 1985. Such protests placed the Alfonsín administration increasingly on the defensive.

Behind the political antagonisms that characterized its relations with the Peronist groups, however, there were some significant indications of a tendency toward compromise. In May 1986, after a number of half-hearted attempts to negotiate a general "social pact" with the unions, the Sourrouille group began to bypass the militant CGT leadership and bargain directly with the key industrial federations, most dominated by old-line Peronists. From the government's point of view, the new approach proved reasonably successful in helping to contain inflationary pressures. Officially designated minimum and maximum wage levels established a range within which wage bargaining would be conducted. Agreements were then negotiated on a sector-by-sector basis, and by the middle of 1986, contracts had been concluded in such key areas as metallurgy, plastics, textiles, and the civil service. Some of these wage settlements added to inflationary pressures, but most of the contracts stayed within government guidelines, and all contained commitments not to seek adjustments for a six-month period—a crucial step for slowing the momentum of the inertial spiral. Although the CGT continued to mobilize protests throughout 1986 and 1987, this round of agreements marked an important turning point in the uneasy relations between the government and the union movement.

A major controversy also arose over the rediscount policies of the Central Bank, headed since 1983 by the Radical economist Alfredo Concepción. To hold the line on monetary policy, Sourrouille sought to limit Central Bank lending to provincial banks that had been hard hit by the financial crisis, but since many of these banks were linked closely to local political machines and small businesses, threats to their liquidity provoked strong protests from the Radical leadership. Conflicts over this issue seesawed back and forth throughout 1985-87. Despite substantial opposition from his own party, Alfonsín backed Sourrouille's effort to gain control of the Bank during 1986 and early 1987. In mid-1986 Sourrouille was able to veto Radical efforts to name new members of the board of directors, and in August he won an even more significant victory when Concepción was replaced as head of the Bank by José Luis Machinea, one of the finance minister's closest allies. For the time being these victories reaffirmed and strengthened the directions charted at the inception of the Austral program.

By the middle of 1987, however, it had become difficult for the Sourrouille group to win such skirmishes. The appointment of a Peronist as the new minister of labor in early 1987 had injected a major note of dissension within the cabinet over Sourrouille's cautious wage policy, and it had become difficult for the administration to resist calls by Radical governors and congressmen for liberalization of Central Bank lending. As with Sarney a year earlier, such decisions appeared to backfire both economically and politically. The approaching gubernatorial and congressional elections of October 1987 made it hard for Alfonsín to sustain anti-inflationary controls, and by the third quarter of the year, annual rates of inflation had edged toward the 200 percent level. The Radicals lost their majority in the Chamber of Deputies and all of the key governorships, and many observers interpreted these losses as primarily a protest against resurgent inflation.

However, in assessing these decisions—as well as the results of the Austral itself—it is important to bear in mind that Alfonsín and his key advisors were operating within an extremely narrow margin of economic and political error. More than in Brazil, local banks and businesses were already contending with extremely high real interest rates and were near the edge of bankruptcy. Whatever Alfonsín did or did not do, moreover, the Peronists remained a powerful force within the electorate—probably a plurality in terms of voter identification.

Finally, the underlying fiscal weakness of the Argentine state—considerably more vulnerable than Brazil in terms of extractive capacity—made it much more difficult for the Alfonsín administration to sustain control of the public deficits. In 1985-86 the price freeze had contributed to deficit reduction by increasing the real value of government revenues, but the gap widened substantially in 1987 in the absence of tax reform and public enterprise reduction. Even during the honeymoon period, however, it would have been extraordinarily difficult for the overextended economic team to design such measures and push them through the Congress, and with the legislative losses of 1987, time appeared to be working against the Alfonsín administration.

Given the magnitude of such challenges, the political and economic accomplishments of the Austral period should not be underestimated. Although the Sourrouille group continued to wrestle with 6–7 percent monthly rates of inflation throughout most of 1987, the Argentines had been considerably more successful than their Brazilian counterparts in deterring a resumption of the inflationary spiral. And if no fundamental problems were solved, the creative combination of heterodox and orthodox instruments allowed the government to steer the system away from crisis without the political and economic devastation of an orthodox shock package. Perhaps most encouraging was the pragmatism and moderation that characterized efforts to put out political brushfires and salvage key aspects of the program. In a political system not known for the flexibility and bargaining skills of its principal actors, these were not trivial achievements. Later in the chapter we will speculate about their long-term implications.

The Return of Politics: State Executives, Parties, and Economic Interests

While aspects of the Austral and Cruzado programs were innovative, they included some important continuities with earlier policy processes in Argentina and Brazil. As we saw earlier in this chapter, the Cruzado decree was not the first time Brazilian authorities had used expansionist policies to dull the edges of distributive conflict. Access to hard currency made such a policy possible—if not through increased exports, as in the mid-1980s, then through ready access to external creditors. Argentina, which has often operated under severe external financing constraints, has periodically attached higher priority to anti-inflationary objectives, as it did most recently under the Austral program.

In past decades both countries suffered destructive economic and political consequences associated with overemphasis on expansion or stabilization objectives. In Brazil, boom periods were followed by external accounts crises and periods of severe austerity (1964 and 1981), and these in turn played roles in changes of regime. In Argentina, both democratic and authoritarian leaders who sought to implement stabilization packages eventually found themselves isolated from their original bases of political support and stalemated by increasing domestic conflict (Wynia 1978). These consequences were frequently linked to changes of regimes and indirectly to long-term deteriorations in basic mechanisms of social control. Are the stabilization efforts described in the preceding sections extensions of these underlying processes, or do they imply long-term changes of direction?

Speculation on such questions requires discussion along several levels of analysis. First, both the constraints on current stabilization policies and the prospects of long-term consolidation and adjustment are influenced by the way state authorities restructure their relations to political parties and labor interests in the transition to constitutional government. Such relations remained parts of the background (although important parts) during the bureaucratic bargaining of the pre-decree phase and the popular euphoria of the honeymoon periods, but they became critical factors in shaping policy later on. In the first part of this section, accordingly, the relations of these political forces are explored in detail. Other major areas for discussion are the business and international environments in which these national dramas have been played out. In the last two parts of this section, we shall explore the changes in these environments which have closed some options previously available to policymakers and opened others.

I. Electoral Politics, the Governing Party, and the Executive Elites

In both Argentina and Brazil the revival of electoral populism was a major aspect of the restoration of party politics. From their inceptions, both the Alfonsín and Sarney administrations encountered strong pulls in populist directions from Radical and PMDB colleagues in their Congresses and statehouses. One of the crucial differences in the implementation phases of the Cruzado and Austral programs was that Alfonsín was better able to shield his economists from popular pressures than Sarney. In part this was attributable to accidents in the timing of crucial congressional and gubernatorial elections following the introduction of their stabilization packages. In Argentina, many important adjustments in the Austral program (e.g., the unfreezing of prices) came *after* Radical party victories in the midterm elections of 1985 and well ahead of the 1987 contest. Sarney, in contrast, faced such decisions in the midst of the campaign for the elections of November 1986. Yet it should be noted that Sarney, unlike Alfonsín, was unable to implement a change of course even after the PMDB's landslide victory in 1986. This reflected important contrasts in the relationship between the president and the ruling party.

The outcome of Brazil's negotiated transition had placed Sarney at a considerable disadvantage. Sarney had attempted to preserve his alliance with the PMDB after his rise to the presidency, but relations between the executive and political majority remained problematic. The president still retained close connections with his colleagues in the Liberal Front, the breakaway faction of the pro-military party he originally led, and he remained on excellent terms with the military establishment (which became an increasingly visible source of support when the Cruzado package began to unravel in early 1987). The PMDB, conversely, had garnered its huge base of support primarily through its opposition to military rule (see Lamounier and Mereguello 1986). Its leaders had acquired national visibility as governors or congressmen during the 1970s and early 1980s, and they were in a position to play a decisive role in the constitutional changes to be drafted in the legislature after the November 1986 elections. In Sarney's view, this seriously limited his freedom of action to adjust the Cruzado, especially during the critical moments prior to the election.

In hindsight, even after taking these considerations into account, Sarney's failure to move quickly on policy adjustments appears to have been a political as well as an economic miscalculation. In mid-1986 his personal popularity was extraordinarily high, and it is possible that if he had capitalized on this strength to back a tough set of demand-containment measures, he might have avoided some of the political problems he faced after November. On the other hand, given the existing correlation of political forces, he might simply have faced a political fire storm sooner, with possibly even more crippling effects on his authority. The rapidity with which Sarney's popularity evaporated after November indicates how thin it had been to begin with. The PMDB might well have been even more likely to dissociate itself from the administration before the election than afterwards. Finally, it is important to note that the pressures faced by Sarney came from both the right and left of the political spectrum. Angry middle-class reactions to the mildly progressive Cruzadinho of July suggest the types of opposition that might have accompanied attempts to shift the costs of austerity upward. On the other hand, not even equitably designed austerity measures were likely to win the support of the left, which had continued its vigorous criticism throughout a major upsurge in working-class living standards. As post-election reactions indicated, the room for presidential maneuver in Brazil was highly constrained.

In Argentina, the transition had created a president with far greater personal authority vis-à-vis the governing party. Unlike Sarney, Alfonsín had been an opponent of military rule, with no prior commitments to the groups associated with the previous regime. There was also less ambiguity in Alfonsín's constitutional mandate: he had been directly elected to a fixed presidential term. Finally, whereas Sarney derived much of his personal power from his association with the PMDB, the Radical party congressmen rode to victory in 1985 on the coattails of Alfonsín, who had a substantially wider base of support than the party.

This did not mean that Alfonsín was free from pressure from rival factions within the Radical majority (Cavarozzi 1986b). In addition to old guard figures long active in the party, there were factions of young "renovationists" who were strongly critical of the cautious economic approaches adopted under Sourrouille. But, for the reasons discussed, Alfonsín had far greater leverage than did Sarney in dealing with such criticisms, which accounts for the weakness of the party backlash against the ouster of Grinspun as finance minister, its acquiescence to the subsequent reshuffling of the Central Bank leadership, and its acceptance of cautious macroeconomic policy adjustments during 1986.

In the long term, the capacity of democratic executives to sustain support for such programs among party and legislative leaders will depend on the extent to which they can construct a consensus over development strategies. Such a consensus requires ongoing consultations, which is difficult to reconcile on a day-to-day basis with the need to insulate technocratic decision-makers from electoral pressures. Yet eventually the most effective way to prevent party elites from making irresponsible populist appeals will be to integrate them more systematically into the policy process.

In this respect the record is poor in both countries. After the sudden introduction of the Cruzado II package in Brazil, the lack of prior consultation became a major issue between Sarney and the PMDB leadership. The costs of administrative isolation and secrecy were not especially apparent in Argentina between 1985-87, but as the regime turns to broad issues of economic reorganization, the need for systematic mechanisms of consultation is likely to become very clear.

II. Unions and the Political Oppositions

Another major issue in the post-honeymoon periods was how to deal with a resurgent popular-sector opposition mobilized by the unions and opposition parties. At the inception of their constitutional transitions, both governments and their political oppositions expressed hopes that broad social pacts on economic policy could reduce the redistributive conflicts that had proved so crippling under previous electoral regimes. But as in earlier decades, government authorities were reluctant to relinquish control over macroeconomic policy, while the labor/opposition groups were too divided internally to collaborate in the imposition of wage restraints. Consequently, despite recurrent efforts to establish negotiating frameworks, state/labor relations remained primarily adversarial with respect to economic policy, with popular-sector organizations conducting vigorous campaigns for expansionist measures at home linked to a unilateral restructuring of external debt obligations. These groups had initially been caught off balance by the popularity of the Austral and Cruzado plans, but as the honeymoons ended, they resumed an intensive round of mobilization and strikes against the general policy directions taken by the new governments.

Surprisingly, Argentine authorities generally fared better than their Brazilian counterparts in dealing with these conflicts. In Brazil, state-labor relations became increasingly confrontational between 1985 and 1987, despite continuing efforts at conciliation by Labor Minister Pazzianotto. In Argentina, on the other hand, where class cleavages had always been more open and intense, the government appeared to be moving closer to a modus vivendi with at least some elements of the Peronist movement.

Several factors helped to account for these differences. In Brazil, unions' expectations had been raised by a prolonged economic boom, and their bargaining leverage had been strengthened both by a massive expansion of the industrial sector and by high levels of employment during 1985-87. This gave major impetus to an unprecedented surge of independent unionism and popular-sector militancy led by the CUT, the PT, and various leftist politicians. In Argentina, the historically strong and militant Peronists faced the reverse situation: lowered expectations, high unemployment, and a reduced industrial sector—all of which created incentives to seek accommodation with the regime in power (Palomino 1986a, 1986b; Pastore and Skidmore 1985).

Government bargaining strategies played significant roles in defining the boundaries of conflicts with the labor opposition. The Argentine effort to negotiate sector-by-sector agreements with key industrial federations was an important turning point in the administration of the Austral package. Arrived at largely through trial-and-error by the Sourrouille group, this approach seemed to point toward a middle course between Swedish-style societal corporatism and unfettered political pluralism. As such it appeared especially well-suited to the task of limiting conflict with Argentina's strong but divided Peronist movement. On the one hand, the decision to bypass Ubaldini's CGT implied a willingness to accept street demonstrations and protest strikes as ongoing features of the Argentine democratic process, and such protests continued through most of 1986. Yet by drawing the heads of the powerful federations into a negotiating framework, the Alfonsín administration was able to obtain agreements within at least some of the "commanding heights" of the economy. Whether such practices could be institutionalized and broadened remained problematic, but for a government that had begun its term in conflict with all segments of the Peronist movement, the overall direction was positive (Cavarozzi, Riz, and Feldman 1986).

In Brazil the general tendency was in the opposite direction. Much of the problem lay in the legacies left by earlier attempts to penetrate organized labor through the imposition of state corporatist controls (Da Silva 1983; Goncalves 1985; Gerschman 1985; Keck 1986). The independent union movement that had begun to challenge these controls in the late 1970s, though popular among rank-and-file workers, lacked a strong organizational base. This left relatively little choice between militant confrontations and the ideals of a broad social pact. Unlike in Argentina, weak industrial federations limited the possibilities for sectoral bargaining, and social pact agreements were impeded by bitter rivalries among competing peak associations. For its part, the government retained control of decree authority and administrative levers, which reduced its incentive to rely on negotiation. Under these circumstances there was little except broad democratic aspirations to contain the mounting conflict between authorities and the labor-based opposition.

Relations reached a new low with the introduction of Cruzado II. On the one side, with little opportunity to influence the decrees of the Sarney administration, the unions increased their reliance on confrontational strategies, with strikes and protest marches leading to violence and direct conflicts with the police. On the other, although the government generally tolerated strikes and protests, it began more and more to respond to such challenges by resorting to tactics reminiscent of the military dictatorship. The attempt to keep wages down by decreeing changes in the inflation index, for example, had been a device recurrently employed in the past by the military, and not surprisingly it was bitterly opposed by virtually every segment of the union movement. Even more ominous was the military decision to occupy port facilities and oil refineries when strikes threatened to shut them down. Such actions served as intimidating reminders of the potential for even more coercive responses to labor protest.

III. Business Groups and the State

For most of the time period covered here, the principal business associations in Argentina and Brazil generally expressed support for the anti-inflationary aspects of the Austral and Cruzado programs as "steps in the right direction," but it did not take long for problems in state/business relations to surface. Portions of the private banking sector were hit particularly hard by restrictive rediscount policies in Argentina and the maintenance of negative real interest rates in Brazil. Argentine industrialists complained of the high interest rates associated with the Austral, while their Brazilian counterparts protested the effects the price freeze and wage increases had on profit margins. In both countries, business elites appeared to be waiting for a clearer picture of intake policies before engaging in major new investments.

Two types of factors were most important in shaping the way business groups defined their interests within their national settings. First was their broad expectations with respect to the "investment climate." Though hard evidence is unavailable, it seems likely that historic national differences in private sector confidence and time horizons were reinforced by the contrasting patterns of political transition in the two countries. As in the past, Brazil's incremental regime change did not fundamentally threaten any major segment of Brazil's capitalist class. Moreover, since much of the Sao Paulo industrial elite had helped lead the transition, it expected to profit eventually from the expansionist policies it had pursued during earlier decades. Conversely, the traditional caution of Argentine capitalists in responding to efforts to encourage long-term investment could only have been increased by the political shocks of the early 1980s. Whether or not the Alfonsín government succeeded in reducing inflation, it faced a much higher "confidence threshold" than its Brazilian counterpart.

Private sector responses to stabilization and adjustment initiatives also depended on the type and scale of investment activities within each business group. In this connection, several useful hypotheses can be derived from Jeffry Frieden's distinctions between the relative weights attached by different business elites to "fixed" and "liquid" assets (see Frieden forthcoming; Maxfield 1986; Schvarzer 1986b). In Argentina the traditional emphasis on liquid assets accelerated during the 1970s as large firms in all sectors of the economy began to shift operating funds into financial markets (Aronskind 1986; Schvarzer 1986a). This probably made it easier for the government to maintain high interest rates as the economy began to revive at the end of 1985 because the larger industrial firms were in a good position to profit from relending activities. On the other hand, the comparative ease with which industrial firms and agribusinesses moved funds across sectors or abroad provided them with a strong source of bargaining leverage vis-à-vis political authorities. To use Marxist jargon, the option of capital flight had made the "upper bourgeoisie" less dependent than state elites on the reproduction of the domestic economic system (O'Donnell 1982: 44-45). This implies a capacity to extract a high price from regimes seeking to stabilize and adjust the economy—in terms of political guarantees and wage constraints. The Austral episode leaves unanswered the question whether such guarantees can be integrated with the types of bargaining relations now evolving in the party and union systems.

In Brazil, the Sao Paulo industrial elite was closely tied to the local economy through its links to state enterprises and public credit institutions. It had concentrated a large portion of its capital in heavy industrial plant and equipment. There was less immediate reason for authorities to worry about capital flight, and there was ground for hoping that industrial elites would respond quickly to emerging opportunities for long-term investment once short-term stabilization problems were resolved.

However, for Brazilian industrialists, more than for their contemporary Argentine counterparts, fiscal and monetary retrenchment imply a contraction of vital sources of credit, markets, and public subsidies, and because their investment in fixed assets has made it harder to leave the system, they have been more inclined—as Frieden suggests—to stay and fight (Frieden forthcoming). For much of the Cruzado period, of course, this was not an issue, since the strengthening of domestic demand and the initial reduction of interest rates appeared to suit the interests of the industrial elite. Nevertheless, elite criticism and defiance of price controls increased during the second half of 1986 as profit margins declined under pressure from rising wages and interest rates. By the end of the year, arguments about the price freeze had broken into the open. In early 1987, after heads of the FIESP (Sao Paulo Industrial Federation) issued well-publicized threats to engage in "civil disobedience" if controls were not relaxed, it became clear that the government could no longer hold the line on the price freeze. Although this *coup de grace* to the Cruzado program stemmed from many factors, it was clear once again that the domestic industrial elite was a major force on the political scene. As in 1981-83 (and earlier periods), it seemed prepared to mobilize against stabilization measures that threatened its interests or to insist that the costs be transferred to other groups within the system. (The implications for Brazil's new constitutional regime will be explored in the next section.)

IV. Constraints and Opportunities in the International System

We can now turn to the changes in the international background against which these domestic conflicts have been played out. Of the major new constraints that have emerged since the early 1980s, the most important for our discussion is the end of any prospects for growth models based on substantial access to private international credit markets. In whatever way existing debt claims are resolved, the banks have made it clear that for the foreseeable future they will not lend "new money" in anything approximating the volumes of the 1960s and 1970s. In addition, the servicing of existing debt has squeezed fiscal resources, exacerbated the strain on domestic savings, and added to domestic inflationary pressures. Finally, increasing developed-country protectionism has raised the barriers to economic adjustments based on increasing exports.

The nature and magnitude of new international opportunities are unclear, but they appear related to the fact that U.S. government agencies and multilateral lending institutions have expanded their roles in the management of international financial and trade regimes. For North-South economic bargaining in general, this has meant a higher priority for strategic and diplomatic interests—a situation more akin to the 1950s than to subsequent decades. For Brazil and Argentina, this has meant greater opportunity to exploit their strategic and economic importance to the United States—as important Third World democracies and as large debtors. How does this mixture of constraints and opportunities affect choices about stabilization policy?

For Brazil, the most serious implication of these new international developments may be the limits they place on its traditionally "developmentalist" orientation. The experience with the Cruzado program indicates that it will be more difficult now than in the past for governments to stretch out boom periods by muddling through external accounts crises. Although the Brazilian economy may continue to expand, growth rates are likely to be lower as a result of contractions in the international economy (whether or not long-term strategies emphasize exports or import-substitution). And even if the external debt is suspended or renegotiated on more favorable terms, governments will encounter more pressure to optimize growth possibilities by confronting short-term issues of stabilization and adjustment. All of this implies more intense political struggles over who should pay the costs.

The "solution" arrived at under somewhat similar conditions in 1964-67 was to transfer the costs of monetary and fiscal austerity onto the wage and salary sector. This course may again appear attractive to the military establishment, upper middle-class, and industrial groups that have otherwise resisted economic orthodoxy. For the time being, this option is limited by military and business commitments to political democracy—although in the past, such commitments have been notoriously tentative (Chalmers 1977). A more enduring impediment may be a workers' movement that appears stronger and more independent of state corporatist mechanisms than in the 1960s. It may still be possible for a military-backed government to intimidate such a movement in order to sustain a wage-repressive stabilization program, but the political costs are likely to be much greater than twenty years ago.

Another possibility is that the mechanisms of political democracy can be used to mobilize backing for a more equitably designed stabilization program, which would shift more of the burden to the upper middle-class and business groups. However, this would present a formidable challenge for political leadership. As we have seen, the upper strata of Brazilian society have reacted strongly against even mildly redistributive adjustments. High expectations on the workers' side would make the task of winning their cooperation more difficult, even with more extensive channels of representation and consultation. Finally, a government seeking to implement a major redistribution of burdens within a democratic context would face the potential veto of a strong military establishment which still claims authority to arbitrate political struggles.

Under these circumstances the power equation appears to point in the direction of a stalemated and inconclusive political struggle over stabilization and adjustment—more characteristically Argentine than Brazilian. Access to official and multilateral aid, debt relief, and underlying economic strength may all provide a sufficient basis for such struggles to be played out within a constitutional framework, particularly if there is moderate expansion in the international economy. This would at least leave open the possibility for political compromise and creative economic problem-solving. But there is considerable risk that stop-go cycles will be shorter and sharper and that the military will not stay far from the surface of political life. On the other hand, a new round of military dictatorship, operating under severe international and domestic constraints, is likely to be more repressive politically and less successful economically than the military regimes between 1964 and the 1980s.

What is true of Brazil might well be considered to apply *a fortiori* to Argentina. All the constraints cited on Brazilian growth—limited access to private credit markets, protectionist barriers to trade, the burden of debt servicing—may weigh even more heavily on the Argentine economy and society. We cannot, therefore, rule out the possibility of new, more intensive cycles of interest group struggle, capital flight, and political turmoil and repression. On the other hand, after so many decades of increasingly self-destructive conflicts, there may be greater incentives in Argentina than in Brazil for cooperative adaptations to new international constraints.*

Argentina may also gain more at the margins from the expansion of the role of multilateral agencies and the U.S. government in the

*I have in mind a line of argument analogous to the hypotheses linking the emergence of societal corporatist mechanisms in small European democracies to their openness to fluctuations in the international system (see Katzenstein 1986).

management of the international financial system. In the competition for official financing, Argentina's evolution toward political democracy counts for more than it would in private markets, while its comparatively weak economy counts for less. Such diplomatic considerations were clearly important in winning U.S. and IMF backing for the original Austral package. Since that time, the Alfonsín government has been careful to cultivate a new image of international "financial responsibility," while official lending authorities have generally continued to adopt a flexible line toward Argentine difficulties. Unilateral debt reductions have repeatedly been disavowed by the Alfonsín government, for example—most recently after the Brazilian debt moratorium of February 1987. Rewards for such behavior included flexible administration of existing IMF standby agreements during 1986 (payments continued despite shortfalls on several targets) and a series of new packages negotiated in 1987. IMF-World Bank agreements concluded early in 1987 totalled $3.35 billion, and included a "Mexican-style" contingency fund to cover slowdowns in expansion. A subsequent $32.8 billion package negotiated with the private bank steering committee covered over 60 percent of the total external debt. It was also reported to include almost $2 billion in new money, as well as a 13-16 percent spread over LIBOR, which had previously been granted only to Mexico on a "one-time only" basis.

Such loans were hardly likely to facilitate an economic miracle, given the domestic and international constraints described above. Nevertheless, as measures aimed at relieving pressure on the declining trade surplus and providing additional incentives to private investment, external financing was potentially a crucial factor in helping to sustain the modest successes of inflation control and growth achieved during the preceding two years. In turn, the domestic policy innovations and political compromises that helped to steer the system away from collapse helped to expand the opportunity to reverse the vicious circles set into motion in the 1940s and 1950s. During that era, zero-sum conflicts at home interacted reciprocally with economic isolation abroad. The democratic accommodations of the present period—reinforced by external assistance—could conceivably set more positive processes into motion.

Chapter Two

THE POLITICS OF ORTHODOXY IN MEXICO

Since the 1940s, the stability of the Mexican political system has been based on a synthesis of two seemingly contradictory historical legacies. The first of these—an outgrowth of the civil war and reforms of the period between 1910 and 1940—is the capacity of the Institutional Revolutionary Party (PRI) and allied sectoral organizations to dominate the electoral arena and mediate class relations. The legitimation provided by the PRI has allowed the governmental elite to combine highly concentrated executive authority with considerable tolerance for public debate and political dissent. The second legacy, originating at the end of the turbulent 1930s, derives from efforts by successive presidential administrations to curb reformist impulses, establish collaborative ties with the emerging private sector, and build a cooperative relation with the United States. Throughout the postwar era, this synthesis provided the foundation for an expanding economy which generated both patronage resources for the governmental elite and extraordinary profits for strategically placed private-sector groups.

The combination of these historical experiences, institutionalized within a framework of one-party dominance and limited pluralism, provides a unique setting for an examination of the politics of economic stabilization. In responding to macro-economic imbalances, Mexico's authoritarian system was presumably less vulnerable to populist challenges than were the new, still fragile constitutional systems that emerged in Argentina and Brazil (Purcell 1973). At the same time, it was also significantly less repressive than the military-based bureaucratic-authoritarian regimes that dominated those South American countries throughout most of the 1960s and 1970s. But the Mexican system has been confronted with a challenge of extraordinary magnitude since the early 1980s. The economic decline that set in at the beginning of this decade has been the worst since the Great Depression of the 1930s, and the orthodox policy responses undertaken under President Miguel de la Madrid have touched a wide range of sensitive social and political nerves. Far more than at any other time in the postwar period, therefore, an analysis of the dynamics of economic decision-making in Mexico must weigh the capacity of the system to manage social tensions against the limits imposed by international circumstances and the conflicting demands of the regime's supporters. To what extent can the regime's strong executive bureaucracy restructure the underlying "social constitution"? How have international pressures and opportunities impinged on policy choices and outcomes?

In this chapter, we will explore these issues in several steps. First, we examine the policies and political balances that underlay Mexico's long period of "stabilizing development" from the mid-1950s to the late 1960s, with particular emphasis on the steps taken under Ruíz Cortines (1952-58) to control external accounts and inflationary pressures that had been accumulating since the end of World War II. The political and economic equilibrium established by these measures provides an essential groundline for understanding subsequent shifts in the Mexican political system—from the reformist efforts of the 1970s to the sharp turn toward orthodoxy after 1982.

In the second section, we focus directly on the initiatives of the De la Madrid administration from 1982 to late 1987. For good or ill, these initiatives have marked an important change in Mexico, and although they are still in process, we will attempt to assess their political and economic scope and significance.

Several kinds of comparisons will be used to highlight the influences at work in Mexican stabilization policy. First, we will compare the way the Argentine and Brazilian governments have handled similar stabilization issues, both in the 1950s and in the 1980s. Second, by focusing both on the 1950s and the 1980s, we can note some useful comparisons across time. How have domestic sociopolitical balances shifted within the Mexican system? What changes in the international system have affected Mexico's relation to it? As we shall see, the decade of the 1980s has presented far more severe challenges than the earlier period. A cross-time perspective provides a measure of these challenges and is thus essential for speculations about the way the Mexican system is likely to ride out the current storm.

Stabilizing Development, 1952-1958

I. Antecedents

The "stabilizing development" measures gradually implemented during the six-year administration of Ruíz Cortines followed a cautious macro-economic policy course that remains highly controversial until the present day. But within the framework of the expanding world economy of the early postwar era, they helped Mexico to achieve one of the highest rates of industrial growth in Latin America, combined with one of the lowest rates of inflation.* To understand the background of these initiatives, we must briefly review three earlier developments within the Mexican system: (1) the shift in the social balance of power following the Cárdenas era (1934-40); (2) the inflation-driven import-substitution strategies adopted by the Mexican administrations of the 1940s, and (3) the emergence of the Bank of Mexico and the Treasury as bastions of financial orthodoxy within the Mexican bureaucracy.

1. In considering the political changes occurring after 1940, it is important to emphasize that Cárdenas's mobilization of workers and peasants left his successors with a dual legacy—a ruling party with a strong popular base, but also a deeply polarized political system. By the time of the oil expropriations and land redistributions of 1938-39, there were sharp divisions both within and outside the "revolutionary family." On the right were the military establishment, emerging business and middle-class groups, conservative northern commercial groups, and U.S. interests; on the left were the newly formed labor and peasant organizations—the Confederación de Trabajadores Mexicanos (CTM) and the Confederación Nacional Campesino (CNC). Although the CTM represented only about 10 percent of the active population, it had become an especially powerful pillar of the revolutionary party, with an armed militia of some 17,000 men and substantial organizational strength in key areas of the economy.

The leitmotif of the Avila Camacho and Alemán years was essentially to bring these union and peasant sectors under control while healing the breach with the more conservative groups. Under Avila Camacho (1940-46), a centrist within the revolutionary coalition, the PRI moved to limit the power of the CTM by dismantling the militias and strengthening the new popular sector within the party for white-

*For different views see Solis (1971), Herrera (1955), Noyola (1956), Caso-Raphael and Miranda (1979, 1984), and Thompson (1979).

collar workers and professionals. At the same time, the settlement of outstanding claims related to oil nationalizations and Depression-era bond defaults helped to reassure conservatives and lay the cornerstone for cooperative postwar economic relations with the United States. The administration of Miguel Alemán (1946-52) moved further and more openly along anti-labor and pro-business lines. The import-substitution policies adopted during this period, essentially an extension of practices initiated under Avila Camacho, provided extensive protection and subsidies for favored industrial and agro-commercial elites while maintaining real wages at low levels (see Table 5). Conversely, on the labor side, the government purged militants from the CTM leadership, consolidated its alliance with union boss Fidel Velasquez, and reduced the peasant sector organizations almost entirely to mechanisms of rural social control (Medina 1978; Torres 1984).

Table 5

Minimum Daily Wage Levels in Mexico, 1945-1966
(In pesos, 1954 prices)

Year	Urban Average	Rural Average
1945	5.41	3.41
1946	5.51	3.56
1947	4.89	3.17
1948	5.25	3.61
1949	4.99	3.42
1950	5.41	3.81
1951	4.79	3.38
1952	5.88	3.99
1953	5.97	4.06
1954	8.22	5.71
1955	7.08	5.78
1956	6.94	5.05
1957	6.56	4.77
1958	6.87	4.96
1959	6.69	4.84
1960	7.60	5.48
1961	7.48	5.40
1962	9.02	6.17
1963	8.96	6.13
1964	11.02	7.80
1965	10.63	7.52
1966	10.60	8.77

Source: King (1971, Table 2.10).

2. The principal objective in the adoption of inflationary development models during the postwar period was to promote the expansion of import-substituting industries (ISI), the preeminent development strategy for most of the postwar era. Since institutional mechanisms for mobilizing public savings could not keep up with the rapid expansion of investment and credit, inflation came to be seen as an acceptable mechanism for the transfer of resources by officials of the Alemán administration (Thompson 1979: 87-89). During the late 1940s, Mexican consumer price increases averaged about 12 percent per year—about the same as in Brazil, and only somewhat lower than in Perón's Argentina (18 percent), where state programs promoted popular consumption as well as industrial investment (Skidmore 1977: 150).

3. Despite this heterodoxy, finally, conservative economists in the Bank of Mexico and the Treasury occupied a distinctive position in the decision-making system. Their influence can be traced to the 1920s when, in the monetary chaos that followed the civil war, remnants of the Porfirian financial system were recruited to supervise the economic reconstruction, establish a sound currency, and restore access to international credit (Anderson 1963). Alfredo Pani, the treasury secretary under Obregon and Calles, became the dominant economic decision-maker of the decade, and the Bank of Mexico, founded under Pani's leadership in 1925, became one of the first and most powerful central banks in the region.* Although opinions within the Treasury and the Bank began to shift away from laissez-faire doctrines after 1929, and by the 1940s many Treasury and Bank officials had come to share in the emerging postwar consensus over ISI, both institutions remained strongholds of monetary conservatism. Toward the end of the Alemán period, they assumed a pivotal role both as critics of the inflationary aspects of ISI models and as leaders in the search for alternative modes of public financing.

External accounts pressures provided the most important stimulus in this search. Although Mexico's comparatively dynamic commercial agricultural sector provided some balance-of-payments relief, postwar domestic demand for capital and consumer imports had led quickly to a depletion of accumulated reserves. In 1948 and again in 1949, this had forced the government into IMF-backed devaluations of the peso, which, in a society tied closely to the U.S.

*The Argentine central bank was purged during the Perón era; in Brazil there was no integrated central bank mechanism at all until 1945 (see Randall 1978).

economy, had unpopular inflationary impacts on import-sensitive domestic prices. With demand for Mexican exports beginning to fall in the 1950s, these inflation/devaluation cycles threatened to become even sharper and more disruptive without some remedial measures. The broadening of exchange controls, proposed by some structural economists, was vigorously rejected by orthodox Mexican economists as unworkable, given the long open border with the United States. This meant, however, that if capital flight and exchange-rate instability were to be avoided in the future, much higher priority would have to be attached to stable prices, the mobilization of domestic savings, and the attraction of foreign capital.

International lending agencies strongly encouraged these views. As previously noted, the IMF had been deeply involved in the currency decisions of the late 1940s, and by about the same time, both the World Bank and the Export-Import Bank had begun to play important roles in the financing of public investment projects. The signals sent by these agencies were clear. A more stable currency would permit Mexico to expand its access to such credits in the future. Significantly, the most active Mexican external borrowing agency—Nafinsa (the National Investment Bank)—was headed under Alemán by Antonio Carrillo, who as Ruíz Cortines's treasury secretary would later become a key figure in the stabilization decisions of 1952-58.

Finally, it should be noted that the effects of inflation on real wages had begun to worry Mexican decision-makers (see Table 5). In part this reflected an economic concern, expressed by Carrillo, that a "further fall in the income of the majority might cause a fall in economic activity" (Thompson 1979: 101), but political considerations also played an important role in the policy process. Since the CTM remained a significant component of the Mexican power structure, Mexican political elites wished to avoid a further erosion in the wages of the unionized working class.

The change in presidential administration from Alemán to Ruíz Cortines in 1952 opened the way for a policy shift in the direction of stabilization. Like the De la Madrid administration thirty years later, the incoming Ruíz government was very concerned about the erosion of legitimacy caused by the flamboyance and corruption of the preceding regime (Pellicer de Brody and Reyna 1978). As in the 1980s, the overarching political motifs were moral rectitude, honest administration, and rationalizing the state's relation to the economy.

Within this general framework, the change of administrations marked the consolidation of the position of the Bank of Mexico and Treasury economists. Beginning with Ruíz and extending through the next two presidential administrations, the three men heading these institutions dominated the policymaking process: Carrillo, head of the Treasury from 1952 to 1958; Antonio Ortíz Mena, Carrillo's successor, who held the position until 1970; and Rodrigo Gomez, the head of the central bank from 1952 to 1970, who defined his principal role in terms of a "struggle to maintain the internal and external purchasing power of the peso" (Thompson 1979: 59). The continuity of the tenure of such men in office was a measure of their power: it contrasted sharply with the revolving door pattern that prevailed in most other parts of the Mexican government. According to Peter Smith (1979), only about 20 percent of all "high office-holders" survived through two presidential administrations between 1952 and 1970; only about 11 percent had, like Gomez, lasted through three (Camp 1972, 1975).

II. Policy Initiatives and Adjustments, 1952-1958

In the 1950s, the high priority attached by these men to financial stabilization conditioned virtually all other policy choices. Within these parameters, however, there was a great deal of experimentation with respect to specific fiscal, credit, and exchange-rate measures. In part this was a product of the need to take into account the interests of key constituencies within the larger political coalition—a process mediated by other members of the cabinet and by the president himself—but it resulted as well from uncertainty within the Treasury and Bank of Mexico about how to pursue their objectives. In this respect, "stabilizing development" policies were best understood not as a coherent package (although later often portrayed in that way), but rather as a series of short-term, rather heterodox responses to the perceived political and economic consequences of earlier choices. The results involved some significant costs (which would become increasingly evident by the end of the 1960s), but the decision-making process also included an impressive measure of learning and adaptation.

Three relatively well-defined policy periods highlight the years 1952-58.

1. Fiscal Austerity: 1952-53. The first step taken by the incoming Ruíz administration was to attack inflation through fiscal retrenchment. Alemán had slowed public investment during his last year in office, but the new administration imposed still further cuts in the construction and public work projects that had previously fueled private-sector activity (Pellicer and Mancilla 1981: 133-35). As a result, prices actually dropped during 1953 (-1.7 percent), and real wages showed an increase. On the other hand, manufacturing output declined (-1.1 percent) (Skidmore 1977: 176), and the overall performance of the GDP (+0.2 percent) was the worst since the 1930s.

In Mexico's comparatively controlled political system, the reaction of organized interest groups was muted and cautious. Nevertheless, strong business complaints about the slowdown, often expressed informally, found their way into the public realm. Statements issued at the annual Bank Association meeting—one of the most influential forums in the private sector—are illustrative. Business leaders complained that "the sharp interruption of our economic progress" was the result of "the way the government had planned and implemented public expenditures." This action, they cautioned, had "created an atmosphere of uncertainty among private investors, who had adopted a wait-and-see policy" (Pellicer and Mancilla 1981: 135).

The response of governmental elites typified general patterns within the political system. On the one hand, the top political leadership closed ranks. Ex-President Alemán, for example, helped to undercut business opposition by publicly endorsing the change in fiscal practices (and then leaving the country). On the other hand, the government made it clear that it was no longer willing to impose a fiscally induced recession to achieve price stability. Toward the end of 1953 the administration began to ease public credit to the private sector, and in 1954 public investments were sharply increased—particularly in electricity, oil, and railroads (*ibid.*, 152).

Fiscal decisions made at this point had long-term implications for the stabilizing development model. By the end of Ruíz Cortines's term, public expenditures were actually significantly higher than under Alemán, and while the public sector share of GDP remained low compared to other countries (Reynolds 1970: 269), it continued to rise in subsequent years as a stimulus to economic activity. Tax revenues remained among the lowest in Latin America, largely because private-sector interests were able to veto revenue measures. A comprehensive income reform was rejected by the president in 1954 as "a measure that would impede the return of a more normal *[sic]* role for private investment in the economic development of the country" (Pellicer and Mancilla 1981: 157). For most of the remainder of the decade, this meant that further efforts at stabilization would have to find a way around ongoing constraints on the state's extractive capabilities.

2. *Fiscal Expansion/Devaluation of the Peso: 1954-55.* As a result of the earlier fiscal decisions, the Mexican economy expanded during 1954 at a rate of 10.5 percent, a postwar high, and in 1955 at a rate of 8.8 percent (see Table 6). Because this expansion took place during a

Table 6

Annual Rates of Growth and Inflation in Mexico, Argentina, and Brazil, 1946-1970
(In percent)

	Mexico		Argentina		Brazil	
Year	GDP[a]	Inflation[d]	GDP[b]	Inflation[d]	GDP[c]	Inflation[d]
1946	6.6%	25.0%	--	17.1%	--	27.3%
1947	4.0	12.6	--	12.2	--	5.8
1948	4.5	6.2	--	13.0	7.4%	3.5
1949	6.1	5.4	--	32.7	6.6	6.0
1950	9.7	10.6	--	24.6	6.5	11.4
1951	7.7	12.6	3.8%	37.2	6.0	10.8
1952	3.9	14.5	-5.0	38.1	8.7	20.4
1953	0.2	-1.7	5.4	4.3	2.5	17.6
1954	10.5	25.9	4.1	3.5	10.1	25.6
1955	8.8	16.0	7.1	12.5	6.9	18.9
1956	6.6	4.9	2.8	13.1	3.2	21.8
1957	7.6	5.8	5.1	25.0	8.1	13.4
1958	5.5	11.5	6.3	31.4	7.7	17.3
1959	-0.1	2.4	-6.4	113.9	5.6	51.9
1960	11.2	4.9	7.9	27.3	9.7	23.8
1961	3.5	1.7	7.1	13.5	10.3	42.9
1962	6.3	1.2	-1.7	28.1	5.3	55.8
1963	5.0	0.7	-2.4	24.0	1.5	80.2
1964	10.2	2.2	10.4	22.1	2.9	86.6
1965	5.3	3.7	9.1	28.6	2.7	45.5
1966	7.7	4.2	0.7	31.9	5.1	41.2
1967	6.5	3.0	2.5	29.2	4.8	24.1
1968	--	2.3	4.6	16.2	9.3	24.5
1969	--	3.7	7.9	7.6	9.0	24.3
1970	--	5.2	4.1	13.6	9.5	20.9

Source: Skidmore (1977, tables 1, 8, 11, 14).

[a] Annual increase/decline in 1950 pesos.
[b] Annual increase/decline at 1960 factor prices.
[c] Annual increase/decline at 1949 prices.
[d] Annual increase/decline in cost of living.

U.S. recession (and hence when Mexican exports were sluggish), external pressures were inevitable. As a result there was a sudden announcement in April 1954 that the peso/dollar exchange rate would be raised from 8.65 to 12.50—the most controversial financial step of the decade. Unlike most such measures, the 1954 devaluation was not a last-resort response to a full-blown crisis. After the preceding period of austerity, reserves remained comparatively high, even though by April the economic expansion had stimulated speculative pressure on the peso. In part (although officials denied it to the IMF), it was a competitive devaluation aimed at increasing sales in the U.S. market. Commodity exports did increase over the next two years, although they declined sharply thereafter (*ibid.*, 165-69). But the primary purpose appeared to be a desire to preempt a balance-of-payments crisis—an objective which was endorsed somewhat hesitantly by the IMF after the step was taken. In the view of government officials, such a crisis was sure to come once the decision had been made to relax fiscal constraints. By acting quickly they hoped to avoid some of the economic disruption associated with the 1949 emergency. Moreover, since it was still relatively early in the presidential term, there was time to recover from the expected political fallout (Thompson 1977: 133).

Not surprisingly, the measure generated significant shock waves. U.S. producers of tradable goods argued (with some justification) that the peso had been *under*valued, placing them at a competitive disadvantage. Within Mexico, speculation against the peso *increased* after the devaluation, leading to a 50 percent decline in reserve levels during May and June (King 1971: 35). Labor unrest was considerable during this period (see below), and despite government controls, domestic prices began to accelerate again over the next two years (see Table 6).

Debates persist to this day among economists and policymakers about whether the devaluation was necessary. Its long-term psychological and political effect was to strengthen official attitudes against such devaluations in the future. For most of the next twenty years, maintenance of the 12.50 exchange rate became a major objective of public policy. However, this increased the importance of finding a way to prevent domestic inflation from disrupting external balances.

3. Debt Management and Inflation Control: 1956-58. During the last years of the Ruíz administration, effective mechanisms for nonrecessive inflation control were finally put into place. An IMF team dispatched to Mexico in 1955 played an important role in helping Central Bank and Treasury officials to formulate aggregate monetary/fiscal targets and "sell" them to other parts of the decision-making elite (Thompson 1979: 139). However, the initiative clearly came from within the Mexican government, and the instruments developed for managing demand were built on well-established foundations: the powerful central banking apparatus and strong links with external lending agencies.

The key domestic measures focused on rechanneling private commercial bank savings toward financing of the public debt. This was accomplished by expanding Central Bank authority to raise reserve requirements (at times reaching as much as 50 percent of total deposits), and to allocate these reserves toward the purchase of government bonds. As a result, between 1954 and 1959 the share of public debt held by commercial banks rose from about 11 percent to over 50 percent, while direct Central Bank emissions declined by a corresponding amount (*ibid.*, 152). To relieve the squeeze on private-sector credit, state investment banks channeled funds into priority industrial sectors, which were also receiving significant tax breaks. Finally, real interest rates were maintained at high levels relative to U.S. rates to help discourage capital flight and stimulate growth in the volume of savings funneled through the private banking sector. Between 1957 and 1967, private bank deposits grew from 15 to 25 percent of GDP (Rivera Ríos 1985: 44).

Since the tax base remained limited, as part of an earlier "bargain" with the private sector, these forms of financing did not alleviate the pressure for significant budgetary restraint. Public support for commercial agriculture—a hallmark of Mexican investment policy during the 1940s—was one of the main casualties. Another was expenditures on health and education, which were low by Latin American standards (Hansen 1971: 85-87). These cuts were part of a continued shift in the distributive balance away from the rural sector and the poor. On the other hand, the state's increased capacity to appropriate private savings allowed increasing levels of public investment to drive the expansion of the economy without an inflationary monetization of the fiscal deficit.

Another vital component of the stabilization strategy of the late 1950s was expanded external financing. From 1955 to 1959, the average annual flow of external public and private credit jumped to over $170 million, compared with a $44.5 million average over the previous five-year period (Pellicer and Mancilla 1981: 54). The acceleration of such flows, both long-term investments and short-term credits, was essential for covering the current accounts deficits that began to widen during the late 1950s. The weight of such flows relative to the fiscal deficit from 1939 to 1976 is shown in Table 7. The portion of the public debt covered by external financing grew from 0.6 percent of GDP in

Table 7

Public Sector Savings, Deficits, and External Financing, 1939-1976
(Percent of GDP)

	1939-46	1947-56	1957-66	1967-71	1972-76
Public sector savings	3.0%	4.3%	3.8%	3.5%	3.1%
External financing	0.3	0.7	1.8	2.2	3.3
Public sector deficit	1.0	1.1	2.3	3.9	5.7
Financed by foreign borrowing	0.2	0.6	1.5	1.8	1.9

Source: Fitzgerald (1978, tables 3, 4).

1947-56 to 1.5 percent of GDP during the next decade. Access to external credit sources built directly on the excellent relations that officials in the Central Bank, Treasury, and Nafinsa had established with such institutions as the IMF and World Bank during the early 1950s, and it was assiduously cultivated in subsequent years. By 1960, Mexico was one of the two or three biggest recipients of World Bank funds, had expanded its access to short-term private credit, and was one of the first developing countries to reenter the international bond market. Subsequently it became one of the major borrowers in the long-term private credit markets that began to open in later years.

Throughout the remainder of the 1950s and the 1960s, the strengthening of the state's internal and external borrowing capacity facilitated an impressive turnaround in earlier patterns. Rates of inflation dropped from an average of about 13 percent in 1946-55 to just under 4 percent in 1956-70 (see Table 6), and earlier cycles of expansion/devaluation were brought to a halt. At the same time the economy continued to expand at a high rate. Annual GDP growth averaged 6.2 percent during 1946-55 and 6.1 percent during 1956-65.

Of course we cannot measure the net effects of the complex economic and political trade-offs which accompanied these gains. As we shall see, some of the choices—the limited tax base, the growing reliance on external debt, and the shift of resources from the rural poor—all laid the foundations of problems that would become important components of crises in the 1970s and 1980s.

From the point of view of the officials in power during this period, however, the gains undoubtedly outweighed the costs. The record of economic growth and reduced inflation, for one thing, contrasted very favorably with experiences elsewhere. Though the Mexican economy did slow down briefly during the late 1950s (coincident with the U.S. downturn of 1958-60), it avoided the deep recessions and balance-of-payments crises which both Argentina and Brazil experienced around 1960. Overall, through the period between 1955 and 1970, Mexican growth rates were far higher than Argentina's and comparable to Brazil's, while its rates of inflation were substantially lower than those in either of the other countries.

In distributional terms, the Mexican formula permitted payoffs to at least some working-class sectors of the governing coalition. Although overall inequality increased, the upper 40 percent of the population (which included much of the organized labor force) did maintain its share of the expanding economy. This contrasted favorably with Brazil, where increases in income shares were limited to the upper 10 percent during a comparable time period.

Most important, despite substantial political and economic strains, to be discussed below, the Mexican system avoided the turmoil and repression that shook so many of the other middle-income countries in the region. The latter, as we have already indicated in the previous chapter, are only now beginning to recover from the wave of bureaucratic-authoritarian takeovers of the 1960s and 1970s.

III. Stabilization and the Political System

How did the stabilization decisions of the 1950s articulate with the broader patterns of relations between the state and organized labor and business groups? One of the distinctive functions of Mexico's dominant party system has been to shield elite decision-makers from electoral or social forces. Consequently, the primary emphasis in our story so far has been on the goals and bureaucratic resources of the economists entrenched within the Central Bank and the Treasury—their strategic position within the executive bureaucracy, their access to international funding institutions, and their command over an unusually sophisticated domestic monetary and credit apparatus (Zysman 1983). We cannot ignore, however, the connections between the inner circles of elite decision-making and the larger balances of power which defined the structure of the Mexican political system as a whole. The authority wielded by governmental elites rested on political alliances and understandings which evolved in earlier decades. The stabilization decisions of the 1950s both reflected and adjusted these alliances. They consolidated not only a macro-economic balance, but also a political equilibrium which persisted until conflicts in the 1970s led to serious new challenges to the policy dominance of the Bank/Treasury elites. In the remainder of this section, we look more closely at the terms of this equilibrium.

The Alliance with Official Unions. In the post-1940 era, two principles governed state/labor relations: (a) the heads of the official union organizations, led by Fidel Velasquez of the CTM, were expected to back major governmental policy initiatives, collaborate in the containment of base-level militancy, and help to mobilize electoral affirmations of support for the system; (b) in exchange, the government guaranteed union officials continued control over their organizations and offered broad opportunities for personal advancement within the party apparatus and in elective offices. Since union officials owed their power almost entirely to the government, their bargaining leverage within this alliance was limited, and they could do little to prevent the long decline in wages that set in after 1940. On the other hand, neither government officials nor union bosses could ignore the wage issue without jeopardizing control over the rank and file, and this provided some basis for union power within the political system. The policy changes of the 1950s reflected the ambiguities of these relationships—relying heavily on the control apparatus to head off labor opposition, but also attempting to consolidate control by reversing policy on wages.

These adjustments unfolded in the context of two waves of labor unrest—the first following the devaluation of 1954, and the second occurring in 1958-59, when the regime confronted rank-and-file rebellions in the teachers' and railway unions. The events of 1954 involved three months of intense general protest against price increases associated with the devaluation, threats of strikes by independent unions, and indications that local affiliates of CTM unions were preparing to break ranks and enter into opposition to Velasquez's pro-government leadership.

The response of the regime and the CTM leadership established the basic pattern for dealing with such pressures throughout the next two decades (Pellicer and Reyna 1978: 83-107; Thompson 1979: 97-107). Although the CTM had not been consulted in advance about the devaluation, the executive council quickly announced its backing for the measure as "a step in the national interest." Rank-and-file pressures mounted during the ensuing weeks, however, as it became increasingly clear that the government could not maintain controls on domestic prices, and after several months of delay, the CTM leadership was finally pushed to a more militant stance. At a congress held in early June, it announced a demand for a general wage increase of 24 percent and threatened to organize a general strike if the demand was not met by July 12. This announcement, however, was the peak of the crisis. Almost immediately the Labor Ministry, assisted by the CTM leadership itself, began working to head off a confrontation through an intensive process of negotiations and settlements in the leading industrial branches. By June 20 over forty agreements had been concluded, and the threat of a general strike had subsided. By July, minimum wages had been raised an average of 20 percent, and out of 50,000 wage demands filed with labor courts, only 150 had resulted in strikes. By September the CTM and allied unions organized massive worker concentrations in Mexico City to reaffirm their political support for the administration and its economic policies.

José Luis Reyna has argued that the successful effort to contain protest over the devaluation marked "a test of fire" for the control mechanisms of the system (Pellicer and Reyna 1978: 102). These control structures were to be tested repeatedly in the future. In the late 1950s, in what is widely regarded as the most serious labor crisis since the war (*ibid.*: 157-215), the government arrested militant activists seeking to gain control of the railway and teachers' unions. Under very different political circumstances, control of official union structures also enabled successive administrations to face down work protests over austerity measures imposed in 1976 and again in the 1980s. In all of these instances, the capacity of the government to rely on the loyalty of dependent union bosses proved a decisive lever of control over civil society.

After 1954, however, the adjustment of the terms of this bargain increasingly involved better conditions and bargaining opportunities for strategically located union groups. Although the huge mass of unorganized workers in the rural and informal/urban sectors remained outside the framework, the general situation of organized workers began to improve. The wage data presented in Table 6 depict the broad trend. Significantly, in the crisis year of 1954 there was marked improvement in wage levels, and the mid-1950s marked an end to the long period of decline. After the labor unrest in the late 1950s, the anti-inflation policies of the government were accompanied by a steady upward climb in real average wages that continued through the mid-1970s.

The State and Business Elites. The understandings regulating the state's relation with business exactly reversed those with the union sector. Whereas the official unions were expected to work with the PRI by mobilizing political support, the post-1940 understanding with business involved an exchange of political power for the right to make money. On the one hand, business elites were expected to refrain from party politics and electoral activity—a norm that was maintained until at least the early 1970s. In exchange, the government deployed its power over the unions and the electorate to promote a "positive investment climate" for favored private-sector groups, which were assigned a pivotal role in postwar development strategies. Finally, although business groups maintained a low political profile, they were offered opportunities to veto major policy initiatives both through extensive informal access to decision-makers and through consultations with formal business organizations such as the Bankers' Association or the National Chamber of Manufacturing Industries (CONACINTRA) (Maxfield and Anzaldua 1987).

Since the inflationary policies of the 1940s had served to concentrate business profits at the expense of wages, industrial elites were at first ambivalent about new policy directions adopted under Ruíz Cortines. As indicated above, private-sector reactions to the fiscal austerity of 1953 were negative. But the understandings worked out in subsequent years regarding low taxes and renewed public investment ended the ambivalence and helped to reaffirm the norms of the earlier partnership. Several aspects of this partnership should be noted here.

First was the pivotal position of the Bank/Treasury economists as the point of connection between private capitalists and the government. The dominance of these economists within the decision-making apparatus substantially expanded business opportunities for consultation over appointments and policy over the two decades. At the same time, the government as a whole moved toward policies aimed at increasing the security and profitability of private investment.

Second, the "sound money" policies elaborated during this collaboration were used to consolidate unorthodox ISI models of growth. Within this framework, conflicts persisted—over the role of foreign capital, and between the more protectionist industrialists of central Mexico and more liberal groups centered in the north. But as in the 1940s, the basis of the highly successful state/business partnership of the stabilizing development period was rooted in the consensus generated by exchanges of political influence and protection rather than in market orthodoxy.

The third important aspect of the evolving partnership was that it involved important structural transformations within the business sector. Priority allocations of public credit, combined with high interest rates and liberalized controls over the movement of private capital, tended to favor large industrial firms and financial conglomerates which could mobilize connections with investment banks or international credit markets. Over the next several decades, substantial concentrations of private liquid capital increased the capacity of business elites to use the possibility of capital flight as a credible threat in bargaining relations with governmental authorities. (We shall return to this point later in the chapter.)

Brazil and Argentina in the 1950s: A Comparative Note. At this point we can gain some perspective on the political underpinnings of Mexico's distinctive course with a brief reference to concurrent responses to stabilization issues in Argentina and Brazil. In Brazil a succession of administrations continued throughout the 1950s to pursue the same type of inflationary growth models abandoned by Ruíz Cortines, until a collapse of access to external credit forced a halt to the process in the early 1960s. On the other hand, Argentina, like Mexico, attempted to implement a major stabilization program in the early 1950s, but it could not be sustained after the overthrow of the Peronist regime in 1955. What factors account for these differences, and what do they imply about the politics of the stabilizing development era?

Brazil's inflationary model rested on the political foundations of (a) a background of good governmental relations with U.S. and local business elites during the 1940s, (b) a weak labor movement under the financial and legal control of the Ministry of Labor, and (c) chief executives selected through a combination of competitive elections and military veto between 1946 and 1964. In these political conditions, it is not surprising that successive governments placed a low priority on containing inflation. On the one hand, for presidents whose tenure was continually threatened by the possibility of a military coup, sponsoring unpopular stabilization packages posed a high short-term risk. On the other hand, the medium-term political costs of inflation were mitigated by the ability of powerful elites to transfer the burdens downward, which was made easier by a weak and dependent union structure. Until the 1960s, finally, exchange controls and external financing alleviated the pressure that domestic inflation placed on external accounts.

Why did Mexico, with even better ties to international sources of external credit, not follow a similar "Avila Comacho/Alemán" pathway into the 1960s? In part as we have already seen, the answer is that Treasury and Central Bank officials were more committed to the goal of monetary stability than their Brazilian counterparts—and probably with more reason, given the prospects of capital flight across the U.S. border. But there were many other Mexican economists and officials who defended inflationary growth strategies during the 1940s and advocated Brazilian-style developmentalist alternatives during the 1950s.

Mexican presidents did not endorse such views, I suggest, because the structure of Mexico's dominant-party system provided them with a matrix of constraints and opportunities that was quite distinct from that of their Brazilian counterparts. On the one hand, Mexican presidents had to worry more about long-term deterioration of wages because the official unions were expected to assist the PRI in mobilizing electoral affirmations of support for the political system. Such incentives were not as strong in Brazil, where state-corporatist unions were supposed to stay out of party politics and maintain a depoliticized labor force. At the same time, since control of the dominant party guaranteed six-year terms, Mexican presidents did not have to worry as much about immediate reactions to unpopular stabilization decisions. With longer time horizons, they could afford to ride out political storms while their advisors experimented with policy alternatives. During the 1950s this provided the space for the incremental evolution of reasonably effective political-economic formulas.

In Perón's Argentina, a highly concentrated system of executive authority also provided the setting for the implementation of a relatively sustained program of economic stabilization after the economy began to encounter severe external accounts constraints in 1949-50. Economists from the more conservative wing of the Peronist movement were placed in charge of the Finance Ministry and the Central Bank and given substantial power over economic decision-making, and as in Mexico, a mass-based party and official union movement, formed during an earlier phase of popular mobilization, served as a powerful pillar of legitimation and social control. Despite an abrupt drop in Argentine wages during the 1950s, the Peronist union movement—like the CTM—tended to stay in line politically.

Why was the Peronist regime unable to consolidate a Mexican-style stabilizing development model? Although there are undoubtedly many reasons, an important part of the explanation lies in the way the timing of popular mobilizations affected opportunities for reconciliation with local businesses and external centers of power. In Mexico, a decade of consolidation preceded stabilization efforts of the 1950s. This established a margin of private-sector tolerance for trial-and-error experimentation, and a framework of understanding within which the state and business groups could work out policy differences. As we shall see, the erosion of these understandings has posed substantial difficulties for the Mexican government in the post-1982 period.

In Argentina during the 1950s, however, the problems caused by the legacy of state/private-sector antagonisms were even more severe. For the Peronist regime, the 1940s had been an era of polarization—not consolidation. In contrast to its Mexican counterpart, therefore, the Argentine government had to confront stabilization issues without having resolved the conflicts unleashed by its earlier populism. Whereas the Mexican governments of the 1950s could capitalize on well-established ties to international credit agencies, Argentina remained outside the Bretton Woods system until Perón was overthrown in 1955. In the meantime, with the political wounds of the 1940s still fresh, the agrarian and industrial elites that dominated the Argentine economy were generally more interested in recapturing political power than in responding to the policy signals being sent out by the Peronist government. Levels of private investment remained low, despite marked improvements in inflation and growth rates during 1953 and 1954, and in 1955—the onset of the halcyon years of Mexico's "alliance for profits"—the Argentine "upper bourgeoisie" was welcoming the military overthrow of the Peronist government itself.

The Political Dynamics of the Stabilization Crisis: 1982-1987

I. The 1970s: Background to the Crisis

Beginning in the late 1960s, partly as a result of decisions taken decades earlier, the political and economic formulas being applied in Mexico began to encounter a number of major impediments. On the one hand, rapid growth during the 1950s and 1960s had generated infrastructural and capital-goods bottlenecks which required urgent attention if expansion was to continue. At about the same time, the system began to show signs of deteriorating political legitimacy, including student protests, sharp declines in electoral turnout, and, perhaps most threatening, an upsurge of guerrilla activity and land seizures in the countryside.

For Mexican elites these developments indicated quite forcefully that significant changes in the prevailing political and economic model were unavoidable, and the turn in more reformist directions—the dominant political trend under Luis Echeverría and José López Portillo—can be understood primarily as an attempt to address the issues from above. Increasing public investment was the principal response to the macro-economic problems, and despite growing fiscal and current accounts pressures, this did contribute to the maintenance of high rates of expansion throughout the next decade. On the political front, both the flamboyant Echeverría and the more moderate López Portillo tried to accommodate a broad range of groups threatening to destabilize the system. Among the most significant initiatives were an acceleration of land reform in the early 1970s, increased investment in health and education, greater latitude for independent unions and collective bargaining, a shift to the left in foreign policy, and a reform of the electoral system aimed at providing greater representation for opposition parties.

Notwithstanding the bitter controversies that flared at various points during these administrations, particularly in the mid-1970s and early 1980s, the reformist efforts were at least partially successful. Without jeopardizing the essential structures of PRI domination, the political spaces opened under both Echeverría and López Portillo helped to deflect or coopt popular groups that were beginning to move in radical directions. This in turn helped to strengthen the capacity of the system to deal with the shocks that were to hit later in the 1980s, but at the cost of upsetting many of the arrangements that had contributed to the stability of the earlier period. For the purposes of our analysis, three sets of developments are particularly relevant to an understanding of the crisis of the 1980s.

1. Fiscal Pressures Associated with the Growth of the State Sector. Although public investment grew steadily in Mexico throughout the 1950s and 1960s, the "shared development" policies announced under Echeverría in the early 1970s marked an important shift in emphasis that carried through to the next decade. As Table 8 shows, the overall

Table 8

Public Sector Growth, 1970-1982

Country	Public Sector Outlays as Percent of GDP		Percent of State Enterprises	
	1970	1982[a]	1970	1982
Argentina	33%	35%	11%	12%
Brazil	28	32	6	11
Mexico	21	48	10	26
Weighted average: Latin America[b]	28	42	9	19

Source: Balassa et al. (1986: 126, table 4.1).

[a]Peak figures for Argentina were 42 percent, for Brazil 35 percent—both in 1981.
[b]Included Argentina, Brazil, Mexico, Chile, Colombia, Peru, Venezuela.

level of public expenditure in Mexico was low in 1970 by comparison with Argentina and Brazil, but by 1981 it had far surpassed those two countries and represented one of the highest levels in Latin America. The state's share of all fixed capital formation, about one third in the 1950s and 40 percent in the 1960s, rose to over 50 percent by the early 1980s, with particular emphasis on petroleum, electricity, and steel (Rivera Ríos 1985: 62; Fitzgerald 1978: 77).

Even more than before, however, inadequate revenue was a serious problem. The Echeverría administration originally viewed tax reform as an essential concomitant of its public investment policy, but efforts to change the tax law were blocked by strong behind-the-scenes pressures from business groups (Solis 1981). Thus high rates of expansion were increasingly accompanied by resurgent inflation, by growing fiscal and current accounts deficits, and by a ballooning of the foreign debt (see Table 9 below). In 1975-76, in the context of bitter controversies over land reform and the change of presidential administrations, a speculative run on the peso contributed to the worst crisis Mexico had experienced in decades, forcing the outgoing Echeverría administration into an IMF stabilization agreement and Mexico's first devaluation since 1954. The onset of the oil boom in 1978 rather quickly resolved the immediate crisis, but had little impact on the underlying structural problems, which remained essentially the same as those encountered in the post-1982 period (Villarreal 1984).

2. *Decline in the Influence of the Bank and Treasury Technocrats.* The onset of the Echeverría period brought an important shift in the correlation of factional forces within the state apparatus and the PRI leadership. Bank and Treasury technocrats remained extremely powerful players in the policy process, but under Echeverría and López Portillo they lost the hegemony they had previously enjoyed. Conversely, structuralists and neo-Keynesian economists played a major role in shaping the shared development doctrines of the early 1970s, and although their influence ebbed and flowed in later years, they continued to have significant policymaking influence until the advent of Miguel de la Madrid in 1982.

Bank and Treasury influence was also diminished by the emergence of new bureaucratic centers of power in the cabinet and within the state enterprise sector. One of the most important such developments was the creation in 1977 of the Secretaría de Programación y Presupuesto (Secretary of Planning and Budget-SPP)—a new superministry with responsibilities for investment planning and public expenditures. Although conservative technocrats often controlled this agency, it tended to tilt in more expansionist directions than the Bank and the Treasury, and on occasion it provided an important platform for economists with less orthodox perspectives (Baily 1980).

3. *The Breakdown of the Social Contract with Business.* An important corollary of these factional struggles within the government was the reintroduction of major uncertainties into the relations between the state and the large business groups. To be sure, the private sector was divided over such issues as trade policy and foreign investment, and its reactions to specific government initiatives were far from monolithic. For example, many industrialists profited substantially from the subsidized inputs and lucrative contracts provided by the expanding state enterprise sector. But business interests in general were uneasy about the new reformist and populist directions taken by the governments of the 1970s, particularly when the decline of the Bank and

Treasury technocrats seemed to be reducing their most important point of access. The general tendency among business groups was thus to expand their political activities and organizational resources in ways that would reduce their dependence on the goodwill of governmental authorities.

At this point special note should be taken of the role played by powerful northern financial-industrial groups linked to organizations such as COPARMEX and CONCANACO.* Although these groups did not speak for the private sector as a whole, they were a major source of pressure in favor of liberalizing trade and capital flows. Particularly after the mid-1970s, they also served as the cutting edge of business demands for greater political power—spearheading publicity campaigns, sponsoring the formation of a major new peak association (the CCE) (Escobar 1987), and providing increased financial backing for the right-wing PAN opposition party, which had begun to grow rapidly in electoral strength in most of the northern states.

Confrontations between these hard-line groups and the government fluctuated considerably during the decade, reaching a high point during Echeverría's land reform in the mid-1970s, and even provoking rumors of a military coup during the presidential transition of 1976. Such tensions quieted down throughout most of the López Portillo administration, but surged again after the economic crisis and bank nationalization of 1982. Even during the quiet periods, however, it was clear that there could be no return to the norms of the stabilizing development era. By the onset of the 1980s, the state-business relationship had become irreversibly politicized.

THE CRISIS OF THE 1980S. Toward the end of 1980, a sharp rise in U.S. interest rates and a decline in the price of Mexican petroleum exports marked the onset of developments that led to the crisis of 1982. For our purposes it is not necessary to determine precisely the relative importance of external and internal causes: clearly both were important. The tightening of U.S. monetary policy—the most immediate cause of Mexico's debt-service squeeze—was beyond the control of the Mexican government, but many of Mexico's policy choices had left the system vulnerable to such shocks. And as the government struggled to sustain the economic expansion of 1980-81, it appeared to compound

*COPARMEX is the Confederación Patronal de la República Mexicana (the Mexican Employers Confederation); CONCANACO is the Confederación Nacional de Camaras de Comercio (National Confederation of Chambers of Commerce).

this vulnerability by allowing the peso to become increasingly overvalued and relying more and more on short-term credits to finance the growing fiscal and trade deficits.

In 1982, the last year of the López Portillo administration, as speculative pressures on the peso intensified, the string finally began to run out. In February, after an outflow of over $1 billion in just three days, the Central Bank withdrew from the exchange market and allowed the dollar price of the peso to double. Next came the establishment of a two-tier exchange market, which established a fixed peso/dollar rate for priority transactions, but an unregulated rate for all others. When such measures proved ineffective, however, the crisis broke into the open. In August, with a "shot heard round the world," the government announced that it would not be able to service the interest payments coming due in the next few days, and began to negotiate a series of agreements with the U.S. Treasury, the IMF, and the private commercial banks. In September, during the final months of the transition period, continued speculation on the peso triggered López Portillo's controversial decision to nationalize the private banking system, evoking another sharp wave of private-sector protest. In early 1983, this initial phase of the crisis was brought to a close with the conclusion of rescheduling agreements with commercial creditors and a settlement with the private financial groups affected by the nationalization decree. The stage was thus set for the new administration to confront the more enduring problems of stabilization and economic reorganization.

These stabilization and adjustment challenges were much more severe, however, than those faced thirty years earlier under Ruíz Cortines. The new problems were not only more intense, but also had different political and economic components. De la Madrid, unlike Ruíz, had to forge stabilization policies in the context of a decade of increasing conflict between the state and capitalist groups, contracting world credit markets, and a sluggish international economy. Whereas Ruíz could build on a broad consensus about import-substitution, under De la Madrid, stabilization was linked to broad revisions of the underlying economic model. Finally, by the 1980s, many of the solutions available to the architects of the stabilizing development period (i.e., low taxes, public investment, and external borrowing) had become important parts of the problem, which raised the stakes of the game for most of the major power contenders within the Mexican system.

II. Political Change and Policy Initiatives: 1982-1987

The inauguration of the De la Madrid administration marked another significant change in the balance of forces within the governmental elite—a strong political resurgence of the technocratic factions associated with the Treasury and the Central Bank, a sharply diminished role for the politicos connected with the PRI and the labor movement, and the virtual elimination of structuralists and neo-Keynesian economists from top levels of the government. De la Madrid himself, a Harvard M.A., had based his career in the Treasury/Bank network, as had thirteen of his eighteen initial cabinet appointees and a large number of subsecretarial and gubernatorial appointees (Hinojosa 1986). The most important of these were the men who filled the three main command centers of the economic bureaucracy—all powerful figures with strong commitments to liberal economic policies. The Treasury went to Jesus Silva Herzog, a Yale Ph.D. in economics, who had initially been appointed in the last months of the López Portillo administration. Miguel Mancera, another prominent orthodox economist, was reappointed as head of the Central Bank after having resigned in protest over the nationalization decree. Finally, Carlos Salinas, whose background had also been in the Treasury, was appointed head of the SPP.

Since the politics of Mexican presidential successions are typically shrouded in secrecy, we can only speculate about the calculations that produced this transfer of power (Sandersen 1983). Clearly, however, the selection of De la Madrid himself, announced in late 1981, already reflected a shift in the priorities attached to economic liberalization and private investment, and by the time his administration took office, it was committed to a comprehensive program of change that differed markedly from the more heterodox and narrowly focused anti-inflation packages described in Chapter One above. The recovery strategy elaborated in the course of the twelve-month transition envisioned a two-step process (Lustig and Ros 1986). The first, to be completed in 1983, was to impose a tough IMF-backed package aimed at reducing inflation, realigning the exchange rate, and stabilizing the pressure on current accounts. This, it was hoped, would quickly establish conditions for an orderly rescheduling of the debt and a rapid resumption of access to new external credit. The second step was to lower trade barriers, diversify exports, and reduce the public enterprise sector—structural adjustment measures which were expected to produce a significant economic recovery by 1984 or 1985.

As we shall see, the actual course of economic events fell substantially short of initial hopes and expectations (see Table 9). After a brutal recession in 1983, there was a brief economic recovery during the following eighteen months, but by 1985-86 the economy again faced recession, escalating inflation, and severe debt-service pressures. Although by the end of its term the government could claim credit for some important achievements—e.g., a big increase in non-oil exports, a buildup of reserves, the establishment of a major stock market—it was clear that a sustained recovery was nowhere in sight. Since so many economic problems were beyond the government's control, it is not easy to say whether alternative policy choices might have produced more favorable outcomes, and I will not try to make an assessment in this study. In the remainder of this chapter, however, we will consider how the government's policy behavior unfolded, the extent to which it pursued its original aims, and the political context in which it occurred. Our first step is to summarize some of the principal features of the policies, grouped into three interrelated categories: stabilization, economic restructuring, and bargaining with external creditors.

1. *Stabilization Policies.* Efforts to reduce inflation and bring external accounts deficits under control can be summarized in terms of several subperiods:

(a) From December 1982 to July 1984, the administration stayed very close to the goals of the IMF agreements signed at the end of 1982. These featured a sharp cut in the fiscal deficit, a contraction in the money supply, and a substantial devaluation of the peso in the unregulated exchange markets. By the beginning of 1984, these measures had led to a marked improvement in the current accounts and to praise from external creditors, but the costs were a 40 percent drop in imports, a contraction of 5.3 percent in the GDP, and a drop in the minimum wage index of about 25 percent.

(b) Between mid-1984 and the gubernatorial/municipal elections of July 1985, fiscal controls were relaxed and the economy experienced a slight recovery. However, as currency reserves declined and inflation continued at high rates, conservative critics began to charge that the government had allowed the fiscal deficit to slip out of control. In September, despite government pledges of new austerity, the IMF announced that it

Table 9

Mexican Economic Performance in the 1980s

	1981	1982	1983	1984	1985	1986	1987
GDP *(annual growth)*	8.0%	-0.6%	-4.2%	3.6%	2.6%	-4.0%	1.0%
Consumer prices *(percent increase)*	28.7%	98.8%	80.8%	59.2%	63.7%	105.7%	143.6%
Urban minimum wage *(1980 = 100)*	101.9	92.7	76.6	72.3	71.1	64.9	55.9
Interest payment on external debt *(as percent of exports)*	29.0%	47.2%	37.5%	39.0%	36.0%	37.9%	27.9%
Fiscal deficit as percent of GDP *(financial)*[a]	14.8%	17.7%	8.9%	8.7%	10.0%	16.3%	
Current accounts *(billions of dollars)*[a]	-$12.5	-$6.2	$5.3	$4.2	$1.2	-$1.3	
Gross fixed capital formation *(as percent of GDP)*[a]	25.7%	22.3%	17.3%	18.0%			
Private	14.5%	12.4%	10.1%	10.9%			
Public	11.2%	9.9%	7.2%	7.1%			

Source: United Nations, Economic Commission for Latin America and the Caribbean (ECLAC), "Preliminary Overview of the Latin American Economy, 1987."

[a]Buffie and Krause (1987).

would suspend the last $900 million installment of the $3.6 billion provided for by its agreements.*

(c) From mid-1985 to July 1986, the economy re-entered a period of contraction comparable in severity to 1982-83. In December the government announced a harsh new austerity package, subjecting new bank credits to a nearly 100 percent reserve requirement and virtually freezing all new credit to the private sector. In January the economy was battered further by a sharp drop in oil prices, and pleas for bilateral assistance were sternly rejected by the U.S. Treasury. In the meantime, despite austerity measures, speculative pressure on the peso continued, inflation headed toward the 100 percent mark, and efforts to reach a new IMF agreement remained at an increasingly bitter standstill.

(d) In June 1986, Silva Herzog—one of the strongest proponents of domestic budget austerity—was suddenly ousted in a bitter bureaucratic dispute with his principal rival, Carlos Salinas. Although this marked no basic change in the government's demand-containment approach to stabilization, the government did attempt to ease the economy out of its recession with a slight relaxation of its credit policies and a new infusion of external assistance. A key to this change was a new IMF agreement on terms sought by the Mexican government. But while these policy shifts helped to dull the edge of the recession, the reactivation was fragile and was quickly reversed by the U.S. stock market crash of October 1987. Growth rates throughout most of 1987 remained near zero, while inflation continued to escalate.

The reasons for these disappointing results were complex, of course, and prompted wide debates throughout the Mexican system. With reference to stabilization policy itself, however, the key issue involved an apparently technical question of how to measure and assess the implications of the fiscal deficit. The deficit had been drastically slashed between 1982 and 1984—from 18 to 6 percent of the GDP—but it began to increase substantially again in subsequent years, triggering a bitter controversy that persisted through the end of the De la Madrid administration. On the one hand, most Mexican officials (echoing their heterodox counterparts in Argentina and Brazil) argued that the

*Suspension of the IMF agreement was announced on the very day Mexico City was hit by one of the worst earthquakes in its history. The timing itself stunned many Mexicans.

deficits were caused by inertial inflation transmitted through the high nominal interest rates required to place government bonds in private financial markets. For them, the appropriate measure of the deficit was the "operating budget" (i.e., with nominal interest rates deleted), which actually showed a slight surplus in 1985 and only a modest deficit in 1986. Many critics, on the other hand, continued to insist on more conventional interpretations which identified the deficit as the principal cause of inflation and high interest rates. Within the government, Silva Herzog was probably the strongest advocate of fiscal austerity—one of several factors that contributed to his ouster. More significantly, concern over the government's fiscal policy led to the suspension of the IMF agreement in September 1985 and to a long period of bitter stalemate that ensued over the next nine months.

We shall return to the implications of this debate later, but in the meantime it is important to note that despite strong political pressure to pump up the economy, the administration stuck quite closely to other key aspects of its stabilization strategy. Private sector credit remained extremely tight, even after the decision to ease up on the brakes in mid-1986. The general thrust of exchange-rate policy was toward prolonged and painful increases in the dollar price of the peso. Wage policy remained particularly tough throughout the period, with the government deliberately lagging wage adjustments behind the escalating rates of inflation. Overall, real wages dropped by about 40 percent during the 1980s—a record comparable to the shock treatments imposed in the southern cone in the late 1970s.

2. *Economic Restructuring: Trade Liberalization and Privatization.* Although the government moved more slowly than it had anticipated in its original plans for structural adjustment, significant changes were made. Several important foundation stones aimed at restoring private-sector confidence and strengthening private capital markets were set in place during the first year of the De la Madrid administration. As noted, the government settled rapidly on compensation to the financial-industrial groups expropriated in 1982. It also offered private firms the opportunity to service dollar debts at favorable rates of exchange, and it permitted the establishment of institutions that many viewed as an unregulated alternative to the nationalized banking system—private brokerage houses (Casas de Bolsa), with wide latitude for financing transactions in domestic capital markets. By 1987 such measures had laid the groundwork for the establishment of the first significant stock market in Mexican history.

With the government facing a severe foreign exchange crisis in 1983, it moved less rapidly to lower trade restrictions. Nevertheless, import authorizations expanded substantially over the next twelve months, and in subsequent years there was significant progress in replacing the cumbersome import licensing system with a more generalized tariff system. By 1985 the proportion of imports covered by licensing requirements had been reduced from 75 to only 38 percent (Lustig and Ros 1986). During the next two years, apparently galvanized into action by the deepening crisis, the government took a number of even more significant steps. In 1986 it signed the General Agreement on Tariffs and Trade (GATT) treaty, ending more than a decade of bitter debate within the business community (Story 1986), and in 1987 it agreed to a major liberalization of bilateral trade relations with the United States. In the meantime—and perhaps most significantly in terms of changes in the structure of the Mexican economy—the peso devaluations of the preceding years had led to a major expansion of non-oil exports, led by rapidly growing investment in the maquiladora plants along the northern border.

The most severe impediment to government plans came in the public enterprise sector, where the major giants proved highly resistant to reduction or restructuring. Throughout the De la Madrid administration, the non-PEMEX (PEtroleas MEXicanos) parastatals continued to place major strains on fiscal resources (4-5 percent of GDP in 1985 and 1986) (Buffie and Krause 1987: 181). PEMEX itself ran surpluses, but its operations proved difficult to rationalize. For example, the government failed to reduce the control of powerful oil workers' unions over subcontracting work conducted for the enterprise—a lucrative source of political patronage (Bortz 1987).

Nevertheless, even in this area there were some signs of movement—significantly more, it should be noted, than in Brazil or Argentina. Popular consumption subsidies offered through CONASUPO (Compañía Nacional de Subsistencias Populares), the public food distribution network, were reduced by over 70 percent in the first three years of the De la Madrid era (Villarreal 1984), and the tariffs for gasoline, electricity, and other services were raised substantially. The government managed to sell or close about 300 medium and small public firms, and at least in some areas proved willing to confront powerful vested interests. In 1986, over the bitter protests of the steel workers' union, it closed Fundidora, the oldest steel complex in the country, and at various points it used unusually strict interpretations of the labor code to crack down on striking electrical workers, telephone employees, teachers, and steel workers in Altos Hornos.

3. *Bargaining with External Creditors.* At the onset of the debt crisis in 1982-83, two assumptions governed the negotiating stance which the Mexican government adopted toward the U.S. government, the IMF, and private creditors. The first was that the risks of confrontation were higher than those implicit in an orderly rescheduling of the debt—a view that continued to guide the government's policy throughout De la Madrid's term. The second assumption was that, with the assistance of external lenders, Mexico's orthodox program of stabilization and adjustment would enable it to re-enter private credit markets and grow its way out of its debt burdens. As the Mexican economy began to enter a new round of crisis in 1985-86, this view began to appear more and more untenable, and from that point onward, Mexico's relations with its creditors began to reflect the tensions between its continued adherence to the first assumption and its changing views on the second. During 1986-87 there were increasing demands for concessions and relief, extracted in difficult, sometimes acrimonious rounds of bargaining with creditors. Yet although the government sometimes appeared to approach the brink during these negotiations, it invariably stopped short of the edge.

The IMF and rescheduling agreements which helped ease the 1986 recession are illustrative of the general process. As noted, these agreements were preceded by nine months of bitter stalemate, and then exacerbated by the shock of the earthquake in September 1985 and the plunge in oil prices the following January. Within the Mexican government, this triggered an extensive debate about the possibilities of a more radical approach to the debt. In March 1986 an internal report prepared under Leopoldo Solis, head of the Council of Economic Advisers, argued that, in the context of the oil shock, it was no longer practical to assume that Mexico could earn external assistance by putting its domestic house in order. On the contrary, domestic inflation would be unavoidable as long as inconclusive negotiations with the IMF and the banks encouraged speculation against the peso. It proposed that the government relax its austerity measures at home, consider bypassing the IMF in its negotiations with creditors, and take unilateral action if it could not reach rapid agreement with the private banks. Treasury Secretary Silva Herzog also began to advocate a tougher position toward creditors in the months preceding his dismissal, but in his case a hard-line external bargaining position was combined with a highly conservative position on the fiscal deficit.

Confrontation was finally averted by the conclusion of a new IMF agreement in July 1986, followed by a rescheduling agreement with the banks a few months later. The specific terms of both involved some unprecedented concessions on the part of the creditors. The IMF, under strong U.S. pressure to head off a crisis, acquiesced to Mexican demands to accept an operational definition of its budget deficits and—in an even more novel step—agreed to peg lending levels to fluctuations in the price of oil. Similarly, in its agreements with the commercial banks, the government obtained an unusually low spread over LIBOR and a commitment for new lending if the economy fell below growth levels targeted for the coming year (*Wall Street Journal*, 23 July 1986, p. 25).

Within the parameters of the existing international debt regime, these concessions represented major victories for the Mexican negotiators, but still unanswered was the question whether they would be sufficient to permit the Mexican economy to do more than tread water during the rest of the decade. Even before the negotiations were concluded, a growing number of Mexican and U.S. economists (some with highly orthodox perspectives) had begun to advocate even more extensive forms of relief—generally in the form of local currency bonds to be paid on a reduced fraction of the total debt.* It should be noted that the debt rescheduling agreement, although signed with the banking committee in September 1986, was not fully subscribed until after the declaration of the Brazilian debt moratorium in February 1987, by which time the government had been forced to scale down its growth targets from 3.5 percent of GDP to a more modest 2 percent figure (*Latin American Political Report*, 12 March 1987). Thus, although the government had shown great skill in playing the game, the issue remained open whether it had not already reached the point where it

*In December 1987 the Mexican government announced a new agreement worked out with the U.S. Treasury and Morgan Guaranty Trust. Mexico is allowed to use dollar reserves to purchase zero-coupon U.S. Treasury bonds at about 20 percent of face value. With Morgan as broker, these are then to be offered at steep discounts to buy back the Mexican loans now being held by the private banks. While it is hoped that this novel arrangement will serve to reduce the size of the Mexican debt, preliminary indications were that the large money-center banks were unwilling to sell back their loans at the 25-50 percent discounts sought by the Mexican government.

might have been worth running the risk of taking an even more radical position.

III. The Politics of Implementation: Control of the Popular Sector

This brings us to the political and economic twilight zone that emerges at the end of every administration—and an attempt to trace the changing power relations that underlay the policy choices described above. A key issue is the extent to which the power of the executive to impose its policies is limited by the need to balance conflicting business and popular interests (e.g., Vernon 1965; Reyna and Weinert 1977)). Perspectives on this issue in the 1980s have been closely linked to positions on the political spectrum. On the one hand, both the administration and its politically liberal critics have emphasized the government's capacity to impose its program—although they strongly disagree about the desirability of the program itself. On the other hand, groups to the right of the government (many business leaders, bankers, multilateral lending officials, etc.) have emphasized performance patterns that can be interpreted as effects of indecision and backsliding—alternating periods of fiscal austerity and relaxation in the stabilization program, periodic concessions to various union groups, hesitancy in opening up the trade regime, etc. Despite the government's orthodox rhetoric (argue these critics), implementation has been severely constrained by the ongoing need to accommodate the PRI's historic popular-sector constituency.

A number of factors make it difficult to assess such arguments. A close look at the day-to-day operations of the De la Madrid government reveals traces of the legitimating balancing act long typical of the system. The issue is not whether such practices continued under De la Madrid, but to what extent—and compared to what standards. This is impossible to measure precisely. The difficulties of gauging shifts in the Mexican power structure are compounded by the degree to which the system shields the intentions and interactions of the principal actors from public view. However, our review of some of the principal features of the government's policy behavior has put us in a position to offer some informed speculation. First we take up the "conservative critique," focusing first on the distributive implications of government policy during the De la Madrid era, and then on the political and institutional levers used to implement them. In the final section of the chapter, we take up the same issues from a different perspective, focusing primarily on the way implementation was shaped by the relations between the state and orthodox segments of the business class.

1. Policy Performance: Backsliding or Persistence? To what extent did the legitimation concerns of the Mexican elite impede implementation of its stabilization and adjustment programs? There are two issues embedded in this question. One is whether the government went far enough and fast enough to engineer a full economic recovery. (I remain undecided on this issue, but it is difficult to resist the impression that the conservatives have set impossibly high standards.) The second is whether the accommodation of popular-sector groups impeded implementation, which can be directly examined by a close look at the distributive, historical, and comparative effects of the policies.

In the first place, it should be emphasized that some of the most difficult problems in implementing the government program were attributable not to popular-sector pressures, but to divisions within the business sector. Import-substituting firms associated with CONACINTRA, for example, were the most important group opposing trade liberalization. In the late 1970s and early 1980s, they had been instrumental in blocking the government's entry into GATT (Story 1986). Similarly, as was the case in many other parts of the world, the sales of public enterprises were limited by the weakness of private capital markets and the lack of private-sector purchasers.

In the meantime, notwithstanding periods of relaxation, the stabilization program weighed most heavily on popular-sector groups. Efforts to lag wages behind inflation were crucial components of government policy, and the sustained decline in real wages contrasted sharply with the stabilization experiences of the 1950s. Cross-national data, though hardly precise, reinforce the general impression that the impact on wages was severe (see Table 10). Although real wages fluctuated substantially in Argentina and Brazil between 1982 and 1986 (and fell off sharply in 1987), workers in those countries appeared better able to defend against inflation—in part because of more open political regimes and more independent unions. Mexican workers in the mid-1980s also seemed to lose ground in relative as well as absolute terms: Lustig and Ros's (1986: 55) calculation of national income distribution in Mexico show wage-earners' share falling from 42.6 to 32.5 percent between 1981 and 1984—a period in which, incidentally,the share of the "foreign sector" climbed from 3.5 to 8.3 percent.

Table 10

Fluctuations of Average Wage in Argentina, Brazil, and Mexico, 1982-1987
(1980 = 100)

	1982	1983	1984	1985	1986	1987
Argentina	80.1	100.5	127.1	107.8	109.5	100.3
Brazil[a]	121.6	112.7	105.1	112.7	121.8	105.8
Mexico	104.2	80.7	75.4	76.6	72.8	--

Source: United Nations, Economic Commission for Latin America and the Caribbean (ECLAC), "Preliminary Overview of the Latin American Economy, 1987."

[a]Rio de Janeiro only.

Within this general context, it is true, the growing fiscal deficits did provide a major source of ammunition for the conservative critique. If, as conservatives argued, expanding public borrowing requirements were driving up inflation and crowding out private investment, this could have accounted for the negative effects on popular-sector wages and employment. But even if one discards the "inertial"counter-argument that inflation and high interest rates were driving up the deficits, it is difficult to pin the blame for the deficits on spending aimed at popular-sector constituents. Both public salaries and public investment declined in real terms after 1982 at rates faster than corresponding private-sector categories. Particularly sharp cutbacks were imposed on health and education expenditures, as well as on consumption subsidies organized through CONASUPO—all items which, during the 1970s, had been considered crucial for expanding the legitimacy of the system. If anything, a far more important source of the deficit was the interest payments on the external debt. They fluctuated between 8.6 percent (1983) and 6.3 percent (1985) of the gross national product (Sachs 1987: 183). In 1986, the last year for which data are available, the figure was 7.5 percent. As a point of comparison, deficits of the non-PEMEX parastatals—another major drain on fiscal resources—were 5.4 and 4.0 percent of the GNP in 1985 and 1986 respectively (*ibid.*, 181). If we are seeking political explanations for the public deficit, one of the main sources would appear to be pressure from external creditors and allied domestic business groups.

Finally, in assessing the continuity of government policy, we must consider some of the roads not taken. From 1982 to 1988, as Argentine and Brazilian regimes became more and more open to popular electoral and union pressures, government policies in both societies moved erratically between severe austerity and very expansionary policies. The Mexican regime, whatever its hesitations or backsliding, resolutely resisted the temptation to experiment with policy alternatives that might, at least temporarily, have brought it greater popularity. For example, although its harsh austerity program had failed to prevent an alarming escalation of inflation in 1985 and 1986, the government continued to rely exclusively on conventional monetary and fiscal instruments, rejecting proposals for wage/price freezes of the type that then appeared highly successful in Argentina and Brazil.* There was, of course, an even sterner rejection of broad pleas for a switch to demand-led growth strategies coming from the CTM leadership and others at the left of the political spectrum. And at a time when Peru had turned to a partial debt moratorium, the Mexican government maintained a strong commitment to meeting its debt service obligations. From this perspective, what appears most striking about the policy behavior of the De la Madrid government was not its shifts of emphasis and tactical retreats, but the consistency with which it stayed within the basic parameters and objectives of its original program.

2. *The Levers of Power.* Now that we have a somewhat clearer picture of De la Madrid's policies, we are in a better position to understand the way the PRI-based political machinery was used to implement them. As in previous decades, the use of party and governmental machinery under De la Madrid involved reliance on both the carrot and the stick to channel distributional pressures, but the mix of these devices and the larger political purpose to which they were put had changed radically during the 1980s. In the 1950s, the presidential authority, party dominance, and the union machinery were all parts of a larger process of re-equilibration of the forces within the political system. In the 1980s, these legitimating mechanisms operated against a backdrop of political disequilibrium and a shift to the right. We can gain a clearer idea of what this implied for popularly oriented currents within the system by examining conflicts within three areas of social control.

*In late 1987, as inflation escalated still further, a wage/price freeze was at last implemented. In keeping with other aspects of past policy, however, wage levels were frozen at extremely low levels, and monetary policy remained very restrictive.

ELITE FACTIONAL CONFLICTS AND PRESIDENTIAL AUTHORITY. As in earlier periods, divisions among contending factions of the elite in the party and the government were held in check by presidential power over appointments and promotions, by shared interests in maintaining the state apparatus, and by ties of friendship and kinship. Because of such integrative mechanisms, political dissent within the elite was sometimes less intense than it appeared to be—an important factor in sustaining the stability of the system as a whole.

Nevertheless, the technocratic counter-offensive noted earlier represented an important change in norms and political practices. In cabinet selections and other appointments, earlier presidents had frequently attempted to distribute top positions among contending currents of the party. In the 1950s and 1960s, for example, the conservative technocrats were confined primarily to the Bank and the Treasury, leaving many political spaces open to groups with alternative perspectives. Presidents such as Ruíz Cortines tended to protect their political legitimacy by remaining above the political fray, cultivating the role of a patrimonial arbiter among contending factions. Perhaps most important, outgoing presidents were frequently succeeded by men representing alternative political currents—which meant that the outsiders of one administration could look forward to a swing of the political pendulum in their direction in the next.

After the seesaw battles of 1971-1982, however, we saw a different pattern emerging under De la Madrid: a president acting openly as a factional chieftain identified with the Bank and Treasury economists, a tendency for technocratic officials to expand beyond the institutional confines of the Bank and the Treasury, and (in late 1987) the selection of Carlos Salinas, one of the dominant figures within this faction, to be De la Madrid's successor. Incoming presidents of Mexico often march off in surprising new directions, but Salinas did not seem likely to alter substantially the economic policy course charted under De la Madrid.

Since these changes led to a more unified, ideologically coherent administrative summit, they contributed directly to the implementation of a highly controversial recovery program. But there were significant political costs attached to the effort to impose coherence and continuity on the top political leadership. The exclusion of rival factions from the upper levels posed long-term threats to the unity of the elite as a whole. With a narrower range of input into cabinet-level decision-making, there was greater risk of political and economic miscalculation and less opportunity to refine policy approaches by testing assumptions about matters such as price controls or bargaining with external creditors. While De la Madrid enjoyed a personal reputation for honesty and integrity (an important improvement over the atmosphere of the 1970s), the "technocratic preferences" he displayed in his appointments and his choice of successor did not help to strengthen the "patrimonial" aspects of presidential authority (Purcell 1973).

CHANGES IN THE STATE-LABOR ALLIANCE. Similar patterns of institutional continuity and political change were exhibited in the structure of laws and patronage relations that tied official union leaders to the PRI and the state. During the 1980s this complex framework of political affiliations, labor courts, and bargaining commissions continued to provide a remarkably effective mechanism of social control that helped to free De la Madrid from the strong union pressures that had become significant elements of Argentine and Brazilian politics under Alfonsín and Sarney.

Yet the severe wage policies adopted under De la Madrid could not have been maintained for so long without substantial shifts in the political terms of the state/labor alliance. From the 1950s through the 1970s, the long-term trend in this alliance had been improvement in both the wages and bargaining leverage of organized labor—particularly for many of the unions that dominated the state enterprise sector. The incomes policy adopted in the 1980s marked a sharp reversal of this trend. Although the administration attempted to provide some relief from the effects of inflation—by reducing the intervals between contract negotiations, for example—its commitment to hold the line on wages substantially reduced the bargaining space allotted to its union allies. In dealing with such powerful public-sector unions as the steel and electrical workers, the administrations of the 1970s had almost routinely used wage concessions to avert strikes. De la Madrid used tough tactics such as dismissal of strike leaders, plant closings, and threats of massive layoffs to enforce labor discipline (Bortz 1987).

There was little that official unions could do to alter these policies, given their dependence on state authorities. As had long been the case, it was the state elite that ultimately established the scope and limits of their political behavior. By the middle of De la Madrid's term, however, the mutual affirmations of support that had once been an important feature of the state/labor alliance had all but ended. Statements issued by the CTM leadership condemned the government's austerity program and called for new policies based on reactivation of domestic demand and unilateral limits on debt payments (Corro 1986). Such statements were generally ignored by the administration. In 1987 the conflict entered a new realm with the designation of Carlos Salinas as the next president. As the head of SPP, the main "spending ministry," Salinas was reputed to be among the most "politically flexible" members of the technocratic team. For the union elite, however, this did not offset the role he had played as one of the principal architects of the De la Madrid program. Having been forced to swallow his presidential candidacy, the labor sector was one of the main losers in the obscure politics of the presidential succession, and it now faced another six-year period with further deterioration of its role within the power structure.

IMPLICATIONS FOR THE PRI. As long as these conflicts continued within the dominant-party structure, they posed little immediate danger to the stability of the system as a whole. De la Madrid's tenure was far more secure than his counterparts in Argentina and Brazil, and there seemed at the time to be little doubt that the PRI would be able to guarantee his choice of a successor. Even so, the conflicts did add to a growing agenda of broad challenges to the party's internal cohesion and electoral hegemony, which reinforced a general impression that the PRI was in trouble and that the system as a whole required political reform.

Until the 1988 presidential contest, the most important opposition challenge came not from the left, but from the right. The former was badly weakened by the lack of financing and by the PRI's control of patronage resources and popular-sector organizations. Meanwhile, the conservative National Action Party (PAN) had the backing of hard-line business factions, and by the early 1980s had begun to make significant gains in the northern states and within the urban middle class. The stabilization and adjustment policies adopted under De la Madrid made it more difficult for the PRI leadership to counter this challenge. On the one hand, the loosening of fiscal and monetary controls prior to the local elections of 1985 evoked vigorous charges of electoral opportunism; on the other hand, the PRI was not helped by the government's decision to tighten its credit policies in the nine-month period preceding the 1986 campaign. Although the PAN's electoral strength was limited to the north, the inconclusive outcome of the voting in that region enabled it to issue strident post-election charges of fraud that were damaging to the PRI's image of electoral invincibility. As the government approached the task of drumming up votes for the 1988 campaign, the electoral picture was further clouded by additional shifts in policy emphasis—from a cautious attempt to reactivate the economy at the end of 1986 to a turn to austerity in response to the stock market crisis of October 1987. Still unanswered was the question whether the outgoing De la Madrid administration would be able to avoid the business-cycle pressures of earlier campaigns, and if so, what the consequences would be for the electoral and party system.

The repercussions within the PRI organization paralleled those already described among the groups in government and union roles. Centrist and leftist activists, many of whom had begun to campaign for a greater democratization of the internal structure of the party, were placed on the defensive. For many such persons, demoralized by the sustained austerity program, the takeover of the party apparatus by technocrats appeared to block opportunities for participation by more politically oriented activists with more extensive connections to the population at large. Their opportunities for influence also seemed reduced by a controversial decision to recruit business leaders as local candidates and party officials—a move aimed at countering the PAN offensive in the northern states. During 1987, dissatisfaction with conservative control of the party boiled over into an internal crisis when a dissident movement headed by Cuauhtémoc Cárdenas (the son of Lázaro Cárdenas) began to call for an open presidential primary. This proposal, which threatened deeply entrenched mechanisms of elite control, was quickly squelched by the PRI leadership. Yet for the orthodox decision-making elites in control of the PRI, such dissent from within the party structure deepened the long-term dilemma of how to reconcile its policy commitments with increasing demands for political reform. Cárdenas eventually bolted the party, and as an opposition candidate in the 1988 presidential contest, he posed the first major left-wing challenge in the history of the PRI.

IV. The Impulses toward Economic Orthodoxy: The Politics of State/Business Relations

Given this damage to the levers of power, why did the De la Madrid administration continue to use them to sustain its stabilization and adjustment policies? What impelled the government to persist for so long on a course that seemed to alienate much of the center and the left without pacifying the right? It is this behavior, much more than the tactical shifts emphasized by conservative critics, that seems most to cry out for analysis. Two possible lines of explanation come to mind—one which emphasizes the interests and beliefs of the decision-making elite and one which stresses the need to fend off the opposition of increasingly militant and independent groups within the private sector.

Undoubtedly the interests and beliefs of the administrative elite form a crucial part of the story. For all their internal political and institutional rivalries, the orthodox technocrats assembled under De la Madrid constituted a remarkably cohesive and powerful decision-making group. Moreover, in implementing its policies the De la Madrid administration showed a significant degree of autonomy from business groups as well as from popular pressures—as evidenced, for example, in the decision to enter GATT and in the severe credit restrictions imposed on the private sector as a whole.

But in several respects this type of "state-centered" perspective seems more useful for explaining the first three years of the De la Madrid term than the last three. Between 1982 and about 1985, there were good reasons to be optimistic about the medium-term prospects of the orthodox Mexican package. The severe recession of 1983 had quickly turned to reactivation in 1984. Creditors appeared pleased, and the Mexican technocrats had received substantial reinforcement from key intellectual reference groups—high-prestige academic institutions, international think-tanks, etc., where orthodox perspectives were in the ascendant.

As recovery collapsed back into crisis in 1985-86, however, matters were not so clear. In addition to the economic setbacks, the orthodox consensus within the international establishment had weakened. The IMF and the U.S. Federal Reserve had endorsed the Austral plan, distinguished U.S. economists were questioning the wisdom of sustaining debt-service payments, and high Mexican officials such as Solis and Silva Herzog were beginning to explore other alternatives. Mexican officials remained deeply skeptical of heterodox "gimmickry," to be sure, and it was not unreasonable for them to continue their basic course. They could still plausibly argue that in the long run their choices would optimize the chances for economic recovery. But by the mid-1980s, with inflation raging, oil prices collapsing, and creditors waiting at the door, the assumptions and certainties of earlier years had been weakened considerably. Since the elite was strongly interested in stability, it would not have been surprising to see it attempting to shore up the political system by turning in somewhat riskier economic directions—maybe not toward the Brazilian (or Peruvian) approaches, but perhaps toward a more cautious Austral-style stabilization plan or toward bolder confrontations with international creditors. We cannot explain why one set of political and economic trade-offs were selected over the other by elite beliefs and interests alone. To account fully for these choices, we must turn to the second line of analysis and situate the behavior of the policymaking elite within the broader context of state/business political relations.

Against the backdrop of the general tensions that had been accumulating since the 1970s, pressure from the northern financial-industrial interests became a source of major concern. This group stood out as the most orthodox and politically radical component of the private sector. On the one hand, with economic and political antecedents that predated the 1910 Revolution, they tended to be less dependent on state protection than enterprises that had emerged in the 1940s and 1950s, more closely allied with multinational firms located in Mexico, and more extensively linked to U.S. capital and export markets. Compared to newer and more domestically oriented interests, they were thus in a reasonably good position to ride out periods of credit austerity and to profit from the liberalization of trade and capital flows.

At the same time, the political radicalism of this group harked back to a tradition of suspicion and active opposition that had marked their relations with post-revolutionary governments during the decades prior to the 1940s. Whereas the more recently formed business sectors usually sought to expand their influence within the PRI-dominated system, the northerners were more inclined to place themselves at the forefront of movements to change the framework of the system itself. Well before the beginning of the De la Madrid administration, the polarization of the mid-1970s had given such efforts considerable momentum. With the post-1982 crisis developing, several additional factors tended to augment their influence and increase their capacity to deter the government from straying far from its original policy course.

The first was the bank nationalization in September 1982, occurring only a few months before De la Madrid's inauguration. Although the new administration rather quickly settled the compensation issues associated with the nationalization, it had several important political repercussions (Luna, Tirado, and Valdes 1987). For one thing, bank owners had previously served as major contacts between state authorities and business firms within their financial networks. Thus the nationalization decree shattered a significant link between the state and the private sector. It also reinforced the hard-line belief that the PRI-dominated system, even when headed by an apparently pro-business administration, could not be trusted to refrain from engaging in "arbitrary" actions. Bank nationalization was the second time since 1975, argued the radicals, that there had been a major assault on private property, and even after the immediate crisis had passed, it placed special pressure on De la Madrid to demonstrate that his administration would guarantee a safe and predictable investment climate.

More generally, the international financial crisis tended to shift the balance of power within the Mexican business community and to increase the leverage that orthodox hard-liners could use against the state. Interruption of the flow of external credit weakened the state enterprise sector as a source of business subsidies and threatened the survival of private firms dependent on public financing and contracts. Much of the northern business class, of course, had fed at the public trough, and at least some of the enterprises within this sector suffered considerably from the contraction. But for reasons already discussed, the northern groups were generally in a better position to turn to foreign markets, to capitalize on alliances with foreign banks and industrial firms, or, if necessary, to get their money out of the country entirely.

Thus throughout the De la Madrid administration, hard-line groups vigorously deployed these economic resources to keep the heat on the administration. Leaders of COPARMEX, CONCANACO, and the CCE, though offering some praise for the government's good intentions, generally sustained a steady drumbeat of criticism against indecision and backsliding, electoral opportunism, or populism. In the meantime the PAN mobilized direct challenges against the PRI itself. The state and local electoral contests of 1985 and 1986 marked particularly bitter moments of confrontation. In demonstrations receiving wide and relatively sympathetic coverage in the U.S. press, PAN supporters occupied bridges, closed stores, and issued angry denunciations of dictatorship and electoral fraud. Though such challenges did not deal specifically with economic policy issues, they reinforced a point made in 1975-76 and in the early 1980s: that militant business groups were capable of mobilizing considerable domestic and foreign support against a government that threatened their interests.

Before proceeding further, it may be useful to pause for a moment and note a puzzling aspect of this business-backed campaign against the legitimacy of the PRI. One must wonder if its long-term result will be to increase both political pluralism and business power, as the hard-liners appear to believe, or whether it will simply help to destabilize a system which, whatever its defects, has offered enormous advantages to the private sector. Particularly in view of the generally pro-business orientations of the De la Madrid government, orthodox hard-liners appeared to be pursuing a strategy which might well backfire badly—not the first time in history that this has occurred. Nevertheless, I suspect that for at least some sectors of Mexico's financial-industrial elite, the risks of political radicalism were less than they appeared on the surface. As I have already suggested with respect to Argentina, the opportunity to transfer capital abroad provides an important form of insurance against the costs of political miscalculation.

From the perspective of Mexican decision-makers, this did not leave a great deal of room for maneuver. On the one hand, the hard-liners' capacity for political disruption was high. At the same time, their economic collaboration appeared crucial to the administration's hopes for recovery. Gaining such collaboration was more than simply a matter of exchange-rate and interest policies: it involved a replacement of the social pact that had broken down since the 1950s—establishing a level of confidence that would coax the investment resources controlled by these groups back into the country and into productive sectors of the economy. In the crisis of 1985-87, this meant avoiding sudden changes in domestic policy or open confrontations with international creditors.

This brings us, finally, to some brief comments about the implications of the government's orthodox policy choices for the long-term stability of the Mexican political system. The main issue is whether such policies can strengthen the material base of the system without fatally eroding the mechanisms of legitimation provided by the PRI. Most neoclassical economists believe that governments responding to contemporary crises of stabilization and adjustment must choose between competing economic and political logics. Political logic, they suggest, may encourage decision-makers to avoid imposing orthodox policies that might lead to a popular backlash, but this will exacerbate existing economic difficulties and lead to greater political instability. Economic logic, in contrast, reflects a longer perspective, and places the rational pursuit of sustained growth ahead of more immediate temptations to cultivate political support. In many instances, no doubt, this view of the policy choices confronting decision-makers has validity, but our analysis of the Mexican case indicates that neither the assumptions nor the policy prescriptions of the neoclassical view are adequate to the complexities of the situation.

First, it was not "economic rationality" alone which led the Mexicans to choose an orthodox approach. Rather, what was at stake was a choice between competing *political* logics: whether to run the risk of alienating the popular-sector base of the PRI by imposing orthodox policies, or to risk the sorts of capital flight and business protests that had posed such difficulties for the system from the mid-1970s onward by not imposing them. The immediate and long-term consequences of each of these alternatives were uncertain. Given the extensive control mechanisms available for containing popular-sector opposition, it is not difficult to understand why business protests might be considered the greater danger in the short run, but it was not clear that the conventional stabilization and adjustment approaches adopted in Mexico would stimulate growth in the long run.

In this connection, it should be emphasized that the economic payoffs for orthodoxy depend in part on somewhat optimistic assumptions about international developments that are well beyond the control of the Mexican government. To a considerable extent, for example, they presuppose maintenance of the liberal parameters of the postwar international economy—a liberal trade regime, access to expanding U.S. markets, favorable interest rates, etc. Of course, even if such assumptions do not hold up, conventional prescriptions for stabilization and market-oriented adjustment may still constitute the "least bad" choice for maximizing growth opportunities. But as the experiences of the 1930s indicate, the application of old policy recipes to new international situations can be counterproductive in the long run. In such circumstances, one might well argue that it is wiser to pursue an experimental economic program which places a higher priority on sustaining the popular legitimacy of the system.

Finally, we must by no means assume that policies which maximize the possibilities of high growth rates will inevitably contribute to the political stability of the Mexican system. To contribute to political stability, economic policies will have to be grounded in extensive renegotiation of the understandings which once regulated conflict within the Mexican system. This will involve establishing a new framework of understandings with the private sector that either neutralizes or accommodates its most radical components, reestablishing a stable framework for trade and credit relations with the U.S. government, and shoring up the regime's deteriorating mechanisms of legitimation by broadening access to political power and material resources. A new wave of economic expansion will not, in itself, resolve these issues. Without attending to the political dimensions of recovery, it could well compound them by raising expectations, disturbing the balance among social forces, and skewing distributive shares.

Chapter Three

DOMESTIC DETERMINANTS OF STABILIZATION AND ADJUSTMENT CHOICES

We can now turn to some of the comparative implications of our case studies. What options are open to Latin American governments seeking to respond to the world economic conditions of the 1980s? What factors have conditioned their selection of particular alternatives? In one way or another, the abrupt contraction of voluntary private lending during the early years of the decade forced austerity on virtually every country in the region. Yet since the general recession of 1981-83, the international policy landscape has shifted many times over, and within that context, the governments of the ABM countries have adopted widely different approaches toward external creditors and domestic adjustment. After working our way through detailed descriptions of several of these policy experiences, we are now in a position to view them from a broader perspective.

Our discussion focuses on the complex role the ABM governments have played at the intersection of the international economy and their respective domestic societies. Over the course of the 1980s, each government has tried to mediate a two-front struggle over allocating the costs of adjustment. Looking outward, it has had to cope with the demands of powerful external creditor groups controlling critical financial resources. Looking inward, it has had to make painful choices among the claims of competing domestic groups and between such groups and the state itself. Not all such choices, to be sure, have involved "zero-sum" conflicts; indeed, most have promised at least some opportunities to share in the gains of economic growth. Even so, in a context of austerity, the struggle over costs and risks has been the most salient component of international and domestic political life.

From the Latin American perspective, the external side of this struggle has presented the most severe constraints. Although local governments have been able to win important concessions on terms of repayment and conditions of external assistance, none has been able to do what the U.S. government has done over the past decade—i.e., shift abroad the costs of low domestic savings rates, large budget deficits, and heavy external borrowing. This asymmetry is reflected in the persistence throughout the decade of net financial transfers out of the region (estimated at about 5 percent of the regional GDP) and in the difficulties which virtually all the countries have had in their attempts to engineer sustained recoveries (Cardoso 1987a: 38).

But the ABM governments did respond quite differently to the distributive struggles occurring within these parameters. On the domestic front, for example, Mexico's sustained orthodox approach shifted much of the cost of adjustment toward the popular sector, whereas more heterodox approaches in Argentina and Brazil sought (with quite mixed results) to reduce these costs or to avoid them altogether. On the external front, there was also a broad variety of bargaining strategies toward creditors—ranging from Mexico's highly collaborative posture in the early 1980s to Brazil's moratorium on interest payments in 1987. In this chapter, we attempt to explain some of these differences in comparative terms. We begin by clarifying some assumptions about the principal actors and the dynamics of the decision-making processes. Next, we step back from the detailed policy focus of earlier chapters in order to identify some of the broader contrasts in domestic and external adjustment strategies. Finally, we discuss some of the political and institutional factors that have influenced these choices—first regarding stabilization and adjustment in the domestic economies, then with respect to bargaining over the debt itself.

I. Actors and Decision-Making Processes: Some Orienting Assumptions

The actors in the national decision-making processes cannot be precisely categorized. Roles blur and subdivide, and individual idiosyncracies weigh heavily in decisional outcomes. Even so, for purposes of comparison, we can identify four types of groups that had important impacts in all three countries: (1) state elites, including political executives and technocrats, (2) the popular sectors, (3) big business, and (4) external creditors.

1. *State Elites: Political Executives and Technocrats.* Since the state apparatuses in the ABM countries are highly differentiated (compared to most other Third World societies), it is useful to refer to top governmental decision-makers as state elites rather than as components of

other political or social groups to which they may also be linked. These elites can be subdivided into (i) political executives (the presidents and their political inner circles) and (ii) the technical advisors who fill the economic ministries, such as the treasury departments and the central bank. The technocrats in the ABM countries came from widely different political and ideological sectors and offered a variety of types of economic advice, but in all three countries, specialized training in academic economics and/or financial management was an important condition for recruitment into the upper levels of the decision-making bureaucracy. This meant that, despite their different political orientations, such advisors possessed credentials which enabled them to enter fully into technical international discourse on macro-economic policy, and that the problems of limited fiscal and financial resources generally figured significantly in their calculations.

Political executives (whether military or civilian) generally placed higher priorities than their technical advisors on maintaining their support coalitions and preserving the legitimacy of their institutional bases. On the other hand, in the day-to-day decision-making process, the political executives had a significant degree of independence from groups outside the government, and they shared with the technocrats a concern about resource constraints that often led to divisions between them and their supporters in the parties, interest organizations, and the military establishment.

2. *Big Business.* This category (the "upper bourgeoisie" in a different language) is made up of the heads of the large private firms and conglomerates—multinational and local—that share economic power with the giants of the state enterprise sector. Among these groups, sectoral differences are important. The most consistent pressures for orthodox policies have generally come from large banking-industrial complexes that were able to capitalize on international credit and market opportunities. Such policies have been opposed, or only reluctantly accepted, by firms with closer ties to the state and domestic markets.

Yet size as well as sector is a critical element in defining the political and economic trajectory of big business groups. By the onset of the 1980s, in the context of relatively modernized industrial economies, these groups had become increasingly set apart from smaller businesses (and from the private sectors of poorer countries) both in terms of the diversity of their economic operations and of their capacity to coordinate their particular interests. They profited enormously from public subsidies, but they were also in a better position than most smaller private firms to operate outside the orbit of state supervision and protection (Frieden forthcoming; Maxfield 1976).

3. *Popular-Sector Groups.* Popular-sector groups are the broad array of parties, unions, and mass movements which compete for the support of blue-collar workers, public and private white-collar employees, and small business owners. Differences in strength and interests of such groups are enormous—both within and between countries. In general, however, they provide the most consistent sources of pressure against orthodox approaches to domestic stabilization and adjustment. I have argued elsewhere that the militancy with which they seek protection from market forces must be understood as a function of their political and economic weakness (Kaufman 1985). Compared to big business interests, they are less able to pass the costs of adjustment on to other groups; they have thus generally suffered the most during periods of retrenchment and have gained the least during periods of expansion. In addition, they are always vulnerable to state manipulation and repression. In the 1980s, therefore, it is not surprising that few in these groups find orthodox appeals to long-term self-interest persuasive.

4. *External Creditors.* Within this category are the public and private institutions that dominate the international financial system: the multinational lenders such as the IMF and World Bank; agencies of the U.S. and other advanced-country governments, including treasury departments and central banks; the large money-center banks and regional banks. An important part of the background of this study is the tugging and hauling among these groups over how to allocate the risks of relations with debtors (Cohen 1986; Lipson 1986; Wellons 1986). Such divisions have at times been adeptly exploited by one or another of the ABM governments. But creditor groups have strong common stakes in preventing the breakdown of the international financial system and forcing the Latin Americans to pay the primary costs of adjustment.

5. *Decision-Making and the Political Process: Uncertainty and Constraint.* For anyone who has closely followed the behavior of these actors in the policymaking process, one of the most striking features is the uncertainty of the day-to-day context in which decisions are made. Even with their relatively sophisticated economic bureaucracies, state elites have only an imprecise quantitative sense of the economic

parameters within which they operate. It is even more difficult for them to gauge the strength of key political forces or to determine their reactions to various policy steps. Among groups outside the government, suspicion and doubt are amplified by the secrecy which surrounds decision-making—which often isolates state elites from their supporters. Finally, it should be noted that high inflation compounds these communications problems. Wildly fluctuating prices impede accurate assessments of resource flows, and competing data on inflation, wage levels, budget figures, etc. are used as weapons of political combat. There is often enormous confusion about who is winning or losing the distributional struggle, even among the participants themselves.

For groups on all sides, therefore, situational cues can become crucial determinants of action and reaction. The choices of decisionmakers are shaped by highly subjective judgments of urgency and opportunity, of mistakes and failures made by their predecessors in office, of growth or decline in their bases of support. To groups competing for resources, the immediate consequences of particular policies may be less important than what they imply about long-term prospects for alliances and political access.

One can argue that such an atmosphere widens the opportunities for either devastating miscalculation or creative leadership (Ascher 1984; Hirschman 1963); in the preceding chapters, we have seen plenty of examples of both. However, we assume that there are outer limits in both directions, established by (1) the structure of the international economy and (2) the socio-institutional cleavages within the domestic political systems.

One limit is posed by the transnational flow of financial and trade resources. Deteriorating reserves, limited international credit, shifts in the terms of trade—all alter the parameters of state decisionmaking and the domestic political struggle. In the pre-1982 era, the tightening of these types of external bottlenecks implied strong pressures toward orthodoxy, although there were major differences in the leads and lags with which governments responded to such pressures. The extension of this type of crisis throughout the Third World since 1982 has partially reduced the risks attached to other options, such as the threat of repudiation of debts. But the point remains that the types of choices available in these situations are objectively different from those available in the boom years of the 1960s and 1970s.

The second limit is shaped by the broad interests which competing groups have in maximizing their gains (or minimizing their losses) in the struggle for resources and power. There is, to be sure, wide latitude in the way in which actors may calculate their opportunities, or in the kinds of alliances they may seek. Even with inflation and political uncertainty, however, we will assume in our attempts to explain policy choices that the perceptions of competing actors will not persist for long in being wildly out of line with reality, either with respect to relative gains and losses or potential friends and enemies.

II. National Responses to the International Crisis: Problem Definition and Dimensions of Response

We turn now to the types of policy choices made in the ABM countries during the 1980s. Figure 6 provides a general summary of responses to three sets of issues. Two of these—macro-economic stabilization and reform of economic structures—deal primarily with the domestic side of the recovery equation. The third issue, that of debt management, involves external adjustments. As a general point of reference for comparing the ABM countries, I have included a stylized summary of the position taken by creditors (mainly the private banks and the IMF) at the onset of the debt crisis in 1982.

An important point highlighted by Figure 6 is that the ABM countries shared a "southern perspective" which at least initially tended to set them apart from their major creditors. No government—not even the orthodox De la Madrid administration—fully accepted the "northern" tendency to pin the blame for the crisis on local mismanagement of domestic demand. All attached much greater importance to fluctuations in commodity prices, as well as developed-country trade and monetary policy—factors over which the Latin Americans had no control. Moreover, while each ABM government adopted a different external bargaining strategy, all strongly challenged the northern assumption that they could grow their way out of debt without substantial new external financing. The crisis was not, they argued, simply a "liquidity" problem: recovery would require much more than the stretching out of interest payments and increases in multilateral lending.

Clearly, however, the ABM governments diverged among themselves in their approaches to these issues. Mexico in particular shared a number of important assumptions with its creditors about the types of domestic adjustments required, while Argentina and Brazil departed more extensively from international norms. Three general aspects of these alternative approaches require comment.

Figure 6

Policy Orientations of Creditors and ABM Debtors Regarding Stabilization, Adjustment, and the External Debt

MACRO-ECONOMIC STABILIZATION	REFORM OF DOMESTIC STRUCURES	EXTERNAL DEBT MANAGEMENT
Creditors	*Mexico and Creditors*	*Creditors*
Problem is excess demand. Solution requires fiscal and monetary austerity, devaluation.	Recovery requires liberalization of import-substituting economy, reduction of state sector and deregulation of trade and capital flows.	Domestic reforms must carry main burdens of recovery. Local efforts to be aided by multilateral lending and rescheduling of private debt.
Mexico	*Argentina*	*ABM Countries*
Same as creditors, but more emphasis on U.S. interest rates and oil price decline as source of problem.	Structural weakness attributable to neo-conservative policies of 1970s. No consensus on liberalization prescriptions. Unimplemented promises to promote exports and reduce size of state sector.	Recovery impossible unless accompanied by new lending and/or debt reduction.
Argentina and Brazil	*Brazil*	*Mexico and Argentina*
Inertial inflation and credit freeze as source of problem. Solutions involve price freeze/ currency reform, with fiscal and monetary controls.	Basic confidence in state-led development models. Ambitious public investment program (Plano de Metas) put on table in 1986.	Attempts to work through IMF to reach agreements with creditors.
		Brazil
		Break with IMF in 1985-87; unilateral moratorium in 1987.

1. The Scope of Domestic Adjustment Strategies. One major difference in the approaches of the ABM governments lay in the comprehensiveness of their plans for reorganizing their economies. The Mexican government—with its strong presidency and well-established technocratic elite—was well ahead of the other two in linking its stabilization program to a broad package of economic reform measures. The Alfonsín and Sarney governments, by contrast, came to power in much more uncertain political circumstances and had less opportunity to look ahead. Thus, although the Austral and Cruzado plans were sometimes portrayed as alternatives to general IMF prescriptions, they in fact focused quite narrowly on only one aspect of economic recovery. In a sense, as Miles Kahler (1986) has suggested, this focus on inflation represented a curious inversion of the heterodoxy of earlier decades. The structuralists of the 1950s and 1960s were frequently criticized for having little to say about how to deal with immediate inflationary problems; the heterodox shock policies of the mid-1980s dealt with little else!

Could Argentina or Brazil have done better with a more comprehensive approach to economic recovery? Despite the constraints under which they operated, Alfonsín and Sarney undoubtedly had some influence on the sequence in which economic policies were placed on the political agenda, and it is worth pausing for a moment to consider the advantages/disadvantages of alternative agenda-setting strategies. On the one hand, it seems plausible that by focusing narrowly on their anti-inflation packages, both governments missed important opportunities to press for reforms with longer-term impacts. What would have happened, for example, if Alfonsín had tried to capitalize on the initial popularity of the Austral by attempting to push fiscal or trade reforms through the Congress in 1985? By the end of the honeymoon period, when tax reforms had become necessary to control inflation, this window of opportunity had narrowed.

But the advantages of a comprehensive strategy are by no means as certain as they may at first appear. With both Argentine and Brazilian societies deeply divided over restructuring issues, premature commitments to broad programs of change might well have undermined support for their anti-inflation packages. And for all their imperfections, these packages did offer some hope of enabling democratic governments to get on top of serious economic crises. In Argentina, the crisis-management efforts were not entirely unsuccessful during the mid-1980s, and it is still possible that in coming years, a democratic government will be able to move toward deeper structural changes. In Brazil, the catastrophic failure of the Cruzado was attributable primarily to the way the program was designed and implemented, and not to a lack of attention to structural reform.

In contrast to the narrow policymaking focus of Argentina and Brazil, Mexico's more comprehensive approach facilitated more consistent day-to-day policy choices. Yet, as Charles Lindblom has argued, the pursuit of "integrated strategies" can sometimes reduce flexible responses to feedback information which indicates the need for adjustments in the overall strategy itself (Lindblom 1965; Lindblom and Dahl 1953; Lindblom and Braybrooke 1973). With recovery still elusive, the big question for Mexico was whether its commitment to a particular direction of change would allow it to recognize when it might be more advisable to change policies than to push ahead.

2. *Orthodoxy and Heterodoxy in Domestic Adjustment.* Aside from their scope, national policies can also be compared in terms of their orthodoxy and heterodoxy—i.e., their contrasting assumptions about the capacity of the state to cushion the shocks of adjustment, and their propensity to experiment with administered solutions to problems of production and distribution. During the mid-1980s, Mexico and Brazil tended to approximate polar positions with respect to such assumptions, while Argentina's more moderate heterodoxy placed it in the middle.

These national differences were reflected most explicitly in the stabilization policies adopted by the ABM governments. Even the limited step of freezing prices, though tempered in the Argentine case by monetary and fiscal caution, deviated sharply from neoclassical assumptions about a government's capacity to manage the economy. The orthodox view was that attempts to administer the price system, even for brief periods, would produce major distortions of the allocative process. It was this concern that underlay the Mexicans' prolonged reluctance to abandon their exclusive reliance on the management of aggregate demand. The proponents of heterodox shock, on the other hand, pinned their hopes on the state's capacity to identify and resolve supply bottlenecks, and eventually on its ability to micro-manage a phased return to market prices.

In principle, such policies might have been combined with more orthodox views on the organization of the domestic economy.* In

*Conversely, relatively orthodox stabilization programs laid the groundwork for state-led development strategies in Mexico during the 1950s and 1960s and in Brazil between 1964 and 1967.

practice, however, despite the absence of fully articulated adjustment strategies, both the Argentine and Brazilian governments appeared to hold ideas about recovery that were quite different from those of the Mexican administration. The approach of the Alfonsín government was shaped in response to earlier disastrous experiences with both Perón's radical populism and the neoconservatism of the Videla years (1976-80). While economic decision-makers were committed to moving toward export-led growth, they were skeptical about the extent to which such growth could be achieved without substantial state initiative and assistance. In Brazil, optimism about the success of earlier developmentalist models led the Sarney government to lean even more strongly in statist directions. Indeed, in the months just prior to the unravelling of the Cruzado, the government unveiled an extremely ambitious public investment program that evoked memories of the Kubitschek years.

3. *External Debt Policy.* Differences in external bargaining strategies are the other distinctive aspect of the ABM responses to the economic crisis of the 1980s. Despite the inability of the governments to halt the outflow of capital, the international bargaining space in which they operated did begin to open up a wide range of options for dealing with creditors. One reason was the increasingly active role assumed by the United States and other creditor governments in the management of the crisis. To avert confrontations with the larger debtors, these governments frequently pressured the IMF and the private banks to show greater flexibility in the conditions they imposed on assistance and debt rescheduling, which provided significant new bargaining opportunities for all three ABM countries. At various points the Latin American governments were also able to exploit creditor attempts to isolate "bad debtors" by rewarding "good" ones. The Brazilian moratorium announcement in February 1987, for example, directly facilitated favorable agreements subsequently negotiated by Argentina and Mexico.

The way each government pursued these opportunities depended primarily on its judgment about the risks associated with confrontation with creditors. These judgments can be classified along a hard-line/soft-line continuum, even though the specific meaning of these labels (like those of heterodoxy and orthodoxy) changed frequently with the shifting terms of the North/South debate.

Hard-line strategies imply (1) greater willingness to break off negotiations with the IMF, private creditors, and other official lenders,

(2) an inclination to publicize confrontations with creditors and mobilize domestic public support against them, (3) a willingness to take unilateral steps to reduce or suspend payments. In Argentina, Grinspun's policies moved in this direction in 1983-84, but after about twelve months he was compelled to abandon his expansionist strategy and come to terms with the IMF. The Sarney government went even further during the mid-1980s. Although the Brazilian government continued to service its debt throughout the Cruzado period, relations with the international financial community were seriously clouded by the rupture of relations with the IMF. Then in February 1987, after expansionist domestic policies had run down its reserves, the government chose to suspend interest payments on its commercial debts rather than adopt more orthodox fiscal and monetary policies urged by the Fund. In Mexico, prior to his dismissal as finance minister, Silva Herzog was rumored to be moving toward a conservative version of a hard-line strategy, in which confrontations with creditors abroad would have been combined with a very stringent form of fiscal orthodoxy at home.

Soft-line strategies stop short of open confrontations with the IMF or private creditors, although they do not preclude tough bargaining behind closed doors. For the most part, notwithstanding widespread sentiment among labor and left intellectuals for the adoption of a tougher stance, this was the strategy adopted by Mexico throughout the 1980s and by Argentina through most of the Austral period. In Mexico it was combined with domestic orthodoxy; in Argentina, with moderate heterodoxy.

III. Determinants of Stabilization and Adjustment Choices: Political Executives, Technocrats, and the Popular Sector

Within the ABM countries, the most politically salient issues confronting decision-makers were generally those related to the stabilization and adjustment of the local economies. Of course, such issues were linked closely to types of assistance available from foreign creditors, and the politics of domestic adjustment could never be completely disentangled from external bargaining strategies. Controversial though they were, however, the burdens of external debt payment were typically less visible than, say, devaluations, credit and fiscal cutbacks, or reorganizations of the public sector and trade. Since the political risks associated with such measures have been quite high, most Latin American governments have been extremely reluctant to impose and/or sustain them.

What, then, has conditioned the varying responses of the ABM governments to domestic stabilization and adjustment issues? As I have made clear, much of the pressure for orthodoxy has come from the international financial establishment and allied sectors of local big business. For the time being, however, we will focus on the way choices have been shaped by the politico-institutional relations between political executives and two other sets of actors: the technical staffs in the economic bureaucracies and the popular-sector forces to which competing political leaders turn for support and legitimacy.

Within the narrow bureaucratic arena, influence flows in both directions between technocrats and political executives. On the one hand, it is obvious that the day-to-day adjustment choices of the political executives turn on the advice of their technical staffs, and the beliefs and predispositions of the technocrats have an important impact on the relative orthodoxy or heterodoxy of the government's approach. The scope of these approaches depends on the extent to which cohesive technocratic elites can deploy their personnel throughout the state bureaucracy. This capacity was highest in Mexico and lowest in Argentina, where incrementalism was to an important extent dictated by the limitations of a small, inexperienced decision-making team.

At the same time, it seems clear that the influence of the technocrats on domestic adjustment policies is even more dependent on the way presidential power structures their decision-making roles. In Mexico, the power of conservative technocrats declined substantially when the presidents of the 1970s shifted their political priorities toward reformist objectives. In Brazil and Argentina, heterodox advisors were recruited from large pools of technocrats in the universities and the private sector, both of which contained far more substantial numbers of orthodox candidates. When the heterodox advisors themselves began to urge caution in macro-economic management, moreover, it was presidential "political calculus" that determined the outcomes.

Although many factors entered into such a calculus, differences in the leverage of popular-sector groups over presidential tenure played a crucial role. The more secure the tenure, the greater was the tendency to follow technocratic advice which emphasized limits on the state's economic resources. Inclinations toward heterodoxy, conversely, varied with the extent to which opposition from popular-sector groups could directly threaten presidential tenure. Typically such threats could be exercised through one of two channels: military backlash against labor unrest or elections.

1. *Fear of a Military Backlash.* In political systems prone to coups, strikes, demonstrations, and other indications of labor unrest can pose serious threats to chief executives seeking to keep the military at bay. James Payne has suggested that labor groups may at times deliberately seek to exploit such fears in order to extract economic concessions from authorities—a form of brinksmanship he labels "political bargaining" (1965). Even when this is not the actual objective of popular protests, executives vulnerable to military backlash have strong incentives to head it off by "caving in" to demands.

Among the ABM countries, the De la Madrid and Sarney administrations were at opposite ends of the spectrum with regard to such threats—with predictable policy results. With his presidential authority firmly established for a six-year term, De la Madrid's virtual invulnerability to a military coup made it far easier for him to sustain the orthodox policies shaped within the economic bureaucracy. Sarney, conversely, was under considerable pressure to reduce union opposition by pursuing an expansionist economic course: his political legitimacy was weak, his constitutional authority unclear, the length of his term undefined. The powerful military establishment had by no means relinquished its self-proclaimed role as arbiter of the political process, and even though popular-sector organizations were comparatively weak in Brazil, hard-line military currents tended to view increasing union militancy as a potential threat to national security.

Alfonsín's moderate version of heterodoxy was consistent with a less immediate military threat. In the long term, to be sure, the armed forces continued to pose a major danger to the constitutional regime, which was dramatically emphasized by the 1987 uprisings against further prosecutions of human rights abuses committed under the dictatorship. But the bitter experiences of the past decade had diminished the military antagonism toward the Peronist unions (a major cause of earlier coups), and the humiliating legacy of the Malvinas defeats had weakened the military cohesion necessary to challenge Alfonsín's incumbency. For the time being, this provided space for the executive to withstand the broad pressure of repeated general strikes and political protest organized by some sectors of the Peronist movement, while seeking conflict-limiting agreements with others.

2. *Elections and Party Politics.* Electoral politics are the other major channel for popular-sector influence. Although general theories of the "political business cycle" have been widely criticized (Alt and Chrystal 1983; Barry 1985), elections do seem to be linked with expansionist macro-economic policies in Latin America. In a study of public spending in seventeen Latin American countries between 1965 and 1975, Barry Ames (1987: 27, 81) found that fiscal expenditures consistently increased in the years preceding elections, particularly midterm contests. With some notable exceptions (the 1985 midterms in Argentina and the 1986 midterms in Mexico), recent experience in the ABM countries has been consistent with these findings. Argentine governments turned to more stimulative policies prior to the 1983 presidential election and again before the congressional elections of 1987. In Brazil, the November 1986 congressional elections played a crucial role in the implementation of the Cruzado policies. Electoral cycles also made a difference in Mexico's dominant one-party system. Efforts to mobilize support for the PRI were associated with an easing of fiscal and monetary policy in the presidential elections of 1970, 1976, and 1982, as well as in the midterm election of 1985.

National differences in the competitive structure of party systems also have an important impact on policy variations *among* the ABM countries. Notwithstanding the weight the Mexican elite attached to electoral legitimation, it is unlikely that its post-1982 wage and credit policies could have been sustained for so long in a more competitive system. On the other hand, with the Alfonsín and Sarney governments facing more problematic tests of electoral support,there was a strong incentive to search for alternatives to orthodox stabilization packages.

Finally, evidence from a variety of countries indicates that executive decision-making is affected not only by the degree of electoral competition but also by the way party structures articulate with electoral rules and frameworks of interest representation. In Europe, societal corporatist institutions have allowed state executives to negotiate the distributive costs of adjustment policies among labor and business peak associations, thus reducing the threat of political backlash (Cameron 1984; Crouch 1984). More recently, Ronald Rogowski (1987: 208) has argued that, in advanced trade-dependent societies, the effects on policymaking of wealth, localism, and zero-sum distributional struggles have been reduced by large electoral districts, list-system proportional representation (which encourages party centralization), and parliamentary (rather than presidential) systems. Against this backdrop, what stands out most about the transitional regimes of Argentina and Brazil was the uncertainty of the constitutional "rules of the game": political actors were still largely feeling their way within an evolving framework of executive/legislative relations, electoral laws, and interest representation. The typical response of executive decision-makers was to attempt to bypass this arena altogether, with secretive bureaucratic decision-making and broad appeals to the mass public. The net effect of such approaches may well have been to increase executive vulnerability to popular pressures.

It is doubtful, of course, that European institutional formulas will provide a magic cure for such problems. Societal corporatist approaches, which rely heavily on peak association bargaining, seem particularly inappropriate to societies where the union movement is deeply divided and there is no strong Social Democratic party to organize a legislative majority.* In a broad sense, however, some of the differences between the Austral and Cruzado experiences indicate the importance of working to establish some kinds of links between executives, party leaderships, and interest organizations. Alfonsín's strong connections to the Radical party leadership provided him with a far firmer political base than his Brazilian counterpart had, and this facilitated cooperative negotiations with segments of the Peronist union movement and the congressional leadership. In Brazil, on the other hand, the loose alliance between Sarney and the PMDB reinforced the penchant to rely on unilateral decision-making and executive decrees, which contributed to a series of disastrous presidential decisions regarding the Cruzado. Stubborn attempts to sustain the price freeze and manipulate the inflation index resulted only in the compounding of initial expansionist mistakes and the alienation of the president from the PMDB and most major business and labor organizations.

IV. Bargaining Over the Debt: Political Executives, External Creditors, and Big Business

Strategy toward external creditors was also subject to the constraints of popular-sector politics. Most union leaders and popular-sector politicians viewed the demands of the IMF and the private banks as major obstacles to their domestic objectives and thus campaigned hard for tough positions on debt repayment. But even for

*See my critique of the "social pact alternative" in Kaufman (1985: 489-92).

governments inclined toward heterodox policies at home, the costs of open confrontations on the external front weighed heavily in the calculations over debt negotiations. Breaks with the IMF meant reduced multilateral lending and greater difficulties with creditors as a whole. The potential costs of sustained defiance of the private banks were suspensions of short-term trade credits, seizures of assets held abroad, and a delayed return to long-term credit markets. During the early years of the crisis, no Latin American government was prepared to run such risks, regardless of the popular pressures it faced at home.

Yet, by the mid-1980s, these trade-offs were by no means so clear. By this point, even the "good debtors" had lost hope for a timely resumption of voluntary private lending, and most were facing a serious new squeeze on current accounts as a result of brief domestic economic recoveries and declining commodity prices. Although increasingly flexible multilateral lending policies began to take up part of the slack, it was no longer possible to ignore the enormous threat that the debt overhang posed to domestic investment and consumption (Lindert and Morton 1987). Under these circumstances, notwithstanding the continuing risks of asset seizures and trade disruptions, a growing number of Third World debtors had decided to reduce or suspend external payments. By 1987 these included Bolivia, Peru, Ecuador, Costa Rica, the Dominican Republic, Honduras, the Ivory Coast, Zaire, and Zambia (Haggard and Kaufman 1987).

Brazil joined this list between February 1987 and March 1988, but considering the changes in the international situation and the growing number of small debtors that had taken unilateral action, the external behavior of the ABM governments during the mid-1980s was surprisingly cautious. On the domestic front, Mexico was a partial exception to broad inclinations to resist orthodox policies. On the external front, the general inclination was to pay the bills—a tendency at work even in Brazil until the moratorium itself.

1. *International Bargaining Opportunities and ABM Policies toward Creditors.* Part of the explanation of the big debtors' caution was their perception that they could use their size and strategic importance to extract better deals from the banks than their neighbors could. In important respects, such perceptions were valid. Private banks did tend to provide special treatment to the ABM countries, both in terms of rescheduling old debts and providing new loans, and the IMF, usually under pressure from the U.S. government, was inclined to be more lenient in giving its approval.

But if these concessions induced moderation in ABM bargaining positions, the overall debt burden might have been expected to encourage them to take tougher positions. According to most of the standard measures of the debt burden, the positions of the ABM countries had worsened between 1982 and 1986 (see Table 11). And in

Table 11

Debt as Percentage of GNP and Exports in ABM Countries, 1981-1986

	1981	1982	1983	1984	1985	1986
Total Debt/GNP						
Brazil	31.4%	36.1%	50.9%	53.2%	49.7%	41.0%
Mexico	34.0	55.5	69.8	59.8	57.5	83.8
Argentina	63.8	83.5	75.9	64.7	60.1	65.8
Total Debt/Exports						
Brazil	297.3	390.2	403.3	348.5	364.2	437.5
Mexico	257.0	311.2	324.9	297.0	326.6	428.1
Argentina	302.2	447.3	461.8	472.6	469.3	533.9
Debt Service/Exports						
Brazil	33.8	43.1	28.6	23.7	25.0	33.2
Mexico	28.1	34.1	40.0	34.8	36.9	36.8
Argentina	18.2	23.8	25.0	25.9	41.9	50.4

Source: World Bank, *World Debt Tables, 1987-88* (Washington: World Bank, 1988), pp. 8, 41, 257.

1985 the debt/export ratios of the ABM countries exceeded both regional figures and those for the IMF list of fifteen "problem debtors."* None of the ABM governments reacted passively to these developments: all attempted to raise the ante of their bargaining demands as their situations worsened. Nevertheless, as I have argued in the case of Mexico, by 1985 and 1986 it would not have been surprising to see even greater bargaining militancy.

The "better deal" hypothesis, finally, is not fully supported by comparisons among the ABM countries themselves. Brazil, which had the lowest debt burden of the three, adopted the most militant stance

*The average figure for Latin America was 295.5 and for the "problem debtors," 284.2. The fifteen countries in the IMF list: Argentina, Bolivia, Brazil, Chile, Colombia, Ecuador, Ivory Coast, Mexico, Morocco, Nigeria, Peru, the Philippines, Uruguay, Venezuela, Yugoslavia (Sachs 1987).

toward creditors, while Argentina, which was in the worst shape of the three countries by far, pursued a relatively moderate bargaining course after 1984. Of course, since Argentina and Mexico had weaker export sectors than Brazil, they were more vulnerable to creditor reprisals—a strong deterrent to hard-line bargaining positions. Yet even greater vulnerability to external reprisals did not stop countries like Bolivia, Costa Rica, or Ecuador from suspending payments on their debt.

2. *The Role of Big Business.* To understand fully the political calculus involved in such bargaining choices, we must also consider the way the (anticipated) reactions of big business weighed in the balance. As suggested above, the groups within this sector generally played a more independent role than their counterparts in the smaller, poorer countries on the default list. Their control over investment resources made their cooperation essential to the success of both domestic recoveries and external adjustments. Indeed, because they could channel the flow of capital across economic sectors or abroad, they were the only domestic social forces, besides the ABM governments themselves, to stand at the intersection of the domestic and international economies. Their reactions or potential reactions to negotiations with creditors were thus critical components of the external bargaining process.

What were the stakes of such private-sector groups in these bargaining relations? On the one hand, even big business did not escape the pressures that debt-servicing placed on private credit and domestic demand, and it shared an interest in alleviating these pressures by reducing external resource transfers. But big business sectors in all three ABM countries also had good reason to be uneasy about hard-line bargaining positions aimed at accomplishing this objective.

Liquid asset holders and export-oriented firms—those most in favor of domestic orthodoxy—stood to lose the most from external confrontations, whereas domestically oriented firms were more inclined to balk at the orthodox stabilization policies usually demanded by the IMF as the price of rescheduling agreements. But even for domestically oriented businesses, confrontations with creditors carried high risks, including the potential disruption of imported supplies and the possibility that hard-line bargaining positions might spill over into politically destabilizing populist appeals at home. The general weight of business opinion thus favored collaborative relations with the private commercial banks.

As the Brazilian experience shows, such opinions were not always effective in preventing governments from adopting hard-line bargaining positions. Nevertheless, I would hypothesize that, as international inducements to soft-line approaches faded in the mid-1980s, the threat of a domestic business backlash became increasingly important in deterring open international confrontation.

The strength of this deterrent varied with the composition of the big business class and the historic context of its ties to the state. A strong financial sector tended to increase the pressure to reach an accommodation with external creditors, as did speculative activities and potential for capital flight. The deterrent to a hard-line position was also affected by historic experiences of class conflict and/or abrupt institutional or policy shifts that reduced "investor confidence." As I have indicated in previous chapters, the need to reassure capitalists seemed particularly strong in Argentina and Mexico, where populist challenges had intensified uncertainties in the relations between big business and the state.

In Brazil, although there was substantial business opposition to the 1987 debt moratorium, pressures against earlier movements in a hard-line direction were considerably weaker than in Argentina and Mexico. One reason was that the dynamism of Brazil's industrial sector had encouraged greater emphasis on fixed-asset investment and reduced vulnerability to capital flight. Between 1976 and 1985, according to one estimate, approximately $10 billion had left Brazil, compared with about $26 billion and $53 billion from the smaller Argentine and Mexican economies (Maxfield 1988). In addition, during the 1970s and early 1980s, populist threats to the business class had been more muted than in Argentina and Mexico, and there was less concern among capitalists about the domestic political implications of economic nationalism.

This did not prevent increasing conflicts between the business community and the Sarney government over the administration's economic populism, and the moratorium decision itself was taken at a low point in the relations between the government and the business sector. Yet the positive basis of state/business relations at the onset of the Sarney era (compared to Argentina and Mexico) gave the Sarney administration considerably more room to maneuver in the handling of the debt issue—and more opportunity to paint itself into a corner. We should recall that the finance minister who led the break with the IMF in 1985—Dilson Funaro—was himself a Paulista industrialist, and business groups harshly criticized the price-freeze associated with his domestic stabilization policy, his confrontation with the IMF received support or only muted criticisms from business sectors until the general economic situation began to deteriorate at the beginning of 1987.

3. *Variations in General Policy Approaches.* The principal themes in our preceding discussion of national policy changes are summarized schematically in Figure 7. The vertical axis distinguishes the extent to which incumbent executives were vulnerable to popular-sector pressure, either through the electoral process or the threat of a military backlash; the horizontal axis distinguishes the degree to which the threat of big business political opposition and/or capital flight hung over governmental policy decisions. For purposes of presentation, we have so far linked domestic adjustment choices primarily to the first set of relationships—i.e., between the state and the popular sector—and external bargaining choices to the second—i.e., between the state and big business. But it should be clear that the choices made by governments in each of these domains continuously conditioned the options available in the other. The four cells of the matrix indicate the main ways in which these choices were combined into overall approaches to recovery. Each combination of domestic and external measures contained its own contradictions, which tended to alter the alignment of political forces on which it was initially based.

Figure 7

Domestic Political Alignments and Economic Policy Choices

GOVERNMENTAL VULNERABILITY:		TO ORTHODOX BUSINESS PRESSURE	
		High	*Low*
TO POPULAR SECTOR OPPOSITION	*High*	**Argentina** *Austral*: Moderate heterodoxy at home: soft-line external bargaining strategy	**Brazil** *Cruzado*: Domestic heterodoxy; hard-line stance toward IMF, followed by moratorium
	Low	**Mexico** Domestic austerity; cooperative relations with IMF and creditors	**Silva Herzog** Greater fiscal austerity at home; hard-line demands for debt relief from IMF and banks

Brazil's placement in this matrix has been discussed at length. The combination of vulnerability to popular pressure and a relatively secure business class induced the Sarney administration to move toward a classical national-populist mixture of domestic heterodoxy and anti-IMF nationalism. Unfortunately (but not surprisingly) this approach backfired, leaving Sarney increasingly isolated from all civilian groups within the political system and more and more dependent on military backing. By the end of 1986, it had become impossible for the administration to prevent a substantial drop in real wages, and although elements of the PMDB supported the moratorium, the government's economic nationalism did little to assuage strong opposition on the left.*

In the meantime, mounting business opposition blocked attempts to shift the burdens of austerity upward: in late 1987, protests from Sao Paulo industrialists over a new price freeze and tax-reform initiatives forced the resignation of the technocrats who were attempting to continue the heterodox course of the preceding years. In early 1988 the Sarney government reversed course, moving toward rapprochement with external creditors and toward a more orthodox domestic stabilization package at home. But in the context of the political stalemate emerging within the Brazilian system, the opportunities for implementing a consistent policy of any sort had narrowed considerably—at least until the end of Sarney's term.

In 1982 the De la Madrid administration faced an alignment of political forces just the opposite of the one initially confronting Sarney: tensions between the government and the private sector were on the rise, while popular-sector discontent was deflected by the control mechanisms of the dominant party. Under these circumstances, Mexican economic policy reversed the path followed in Brazil: it was the most orthodox of the three countries with respect to domestic adjustments and, notwithstanding some tense moments with creditors, the most soft-line abroad. Like Sarney's national-populist approach, however, the conservative recovery strategy mounted in Mexico carried a high political cost, contributing to a severe erosion of the PRI's popular support and an unprecedented challenge from the left in the

*The reaction of Brazilian labor leader Luís Ignacio Lula da Silva captures the attitude of much of the left: "The moratorium is not a proof of the government's strength. The only thing it shows is that the government is broke" (*Veja*, 25 February 1987, p. 34). A wide range of negative business reactions are reviewed in the same issue.

1988 presidential elections. The next administration may well change its policy substantially in response to these developments. If it does not, Mexico could experience a sociopolitical stalemate not unlike the one threatening Brazil, with a government isolated from both labor and business and increasingly dependent on the military establishment for support.

A third type of situation confronted Alfonsín's new government as it entered office: a long history of severe class and sectoral conflicts, and intense pressure on the government from *both* orthodox business and popular groups. The Austral package can be viewed as an attempt to steer the system away from these cross-pressures by combining moderate heterodoxy at home with a relatively collaborative stance toward international creditors. The outcome of this experiment indicated that while incremental progress was possible, it was not easy to sustain a viable balance among the contending political forces. The government's innovative stabilization approach managed to reduce inflation without imposing an orthodox shock treatment, but deep political divisions among Peronists and Alfonsín's own Radical party made it difficult to build on this initial success with further economic reforms. At the same time, although both external creditors and local businesses responded with some flexibility to price controls and currency reforms, they proved unwilling to provide the external resources and domestic investment necessary for full economic recovery.

What are the long-run political and economic implications of this experience? On the one hand, notwithstanding their frustration with the state of the Argentine economy, the major Argentine power groups continue to prefer the contemporary constitutional system to the repressive and adventuristic military dictatorship that preceded it. This means that, for the time being, the survival of Argentine democracy will not depend on the success of programs such as the Austral. On the other hand, the possibility of sustained economic recovery—one not undermined by political polarization and changes of regime—will require the continuation of democratic opportunities for contending groups to participate in, and learn from, the processes of economic decision-making. The Austral program, which was adopted after the failure of more populist policies, provides an important example of incremental learning. Although subsequent Peronist or Radical administrations might repeat many of Alfonsín's early mistakes, it is possible that they also might grow in economic realism and creativity as they cope with the challenges of governmental responsibility. For such learning cycles to expand, democratic commitments must hold firm through subsequent periods of economic difficulty, and the international system must provide opportunities for adjustment.

Like the Austral package, the fourth policy approach indicated in Figure 7—one which so far has not been tried in the ABM countries—involves an unusual combination of foreign and domestic economic policies: orthodox fiscal and monetary policies at home, but a significant reduction in external debt burdens to be effected (if necessary) through a unilateral redefinition of obligations to creditors. Such an approach, which assumes the need for painful adjustments both domestically and abroad, seems logical. But what sorts of political circumstances would be needed to make it feasible in the ABM countries?

Unless it led very quickly to economic recovery—a doubtful possibility given the likelihood of a negative reaction from external creditors—such an orthodox/hard-line approach could probably not be sustained in a context of democratic pluralism and competitive elections. Economic nationalism might blunt popular reactions to domestic austerity, but not enough to avoid the need for some sorts of limits on political opposition. On the other hand, an authoritarian regime which attempted to pursue a hard-line external bargaining policy would have to be quite different from the bureaucratic-authoritarian regimes of the 1960s and 1970s which sought the support of international financial groups.

The closest historical analogies that come to mind are the Brazilian Estado Novo of the 1930s and the Mexican system under Miguel Alemán in the 1940s. In each case, the government combined economic nationalism and support for local industrialists with severely restrictive policies toward labor. Yet these coalitions were formed in domestic and international contexts very different from the present, with local economies in the process of import-substitution industrialization and local businesses still requiring substantial state tutelage and support. It would be far more difficult to construct a nationalist but pro-business coalition in the 1980s, a time when the primary challenge appears to be one of reorienting the economy in more outward directions.

Conceivably a figure such as Silva Herzog, who had wide prestige in the business sector and some political ties to the left, might have been able to implement a hard-line/orthodox program long enough to redefine the terms of Mexico's relations to external creditors and make the necessary adjustments in the local economy. But this would have threatened authorities with isolation from most major domestic and international forces, implying a degree of state autonomy not present in any of the ABM countries. Under such circumstances, it should not be surprising that the orthodox/hard-line approach has so far remained a road not taken.

REFERENCES

Alt, James A., and Chrystal, K. Alec. 1983. *Political Economics.* Berkeley: University of California Press.

Ames, Barry. 1987. *Politics of Survival: Politicians and Public Policy in Latin America.* Berkeley: University of California Press.

Anderson, Charles W. 1963. "Bankers as Revolutionaries: Politics and Development Banking in Mexico." In *The Political Economy of Mexico,* eds. William P. Glade and C.W. Anderson. Madison: University of Wisconsin Press.

Arido, Persio, and Lara-Resende, André. 1985. "Inertial Inflation and Monetary Reform: Brazil." In Williamson, ed.

Aronskind, Ricardo. 1986. "Capitalización en las empresas locales." *El Bimestre* 36, 2.

Ascher, William. 1984. *Scheming for the Poor.* Cambridge, Mass.: Harvard University Press.

Baer, Werner. 1965. *Industrialization and Economic Development in Brazil.* Homewood, IL.: Economic Growth Center, Yale University.

Baer, Werner, and Kerstenetzky, Isaac. 1964. *Inflation and Growth in Latin America.* Homewood, IL.: Richard D. Irwin.

Baily, John J. 1980. "Presidency, Bureaucracy, and Administrative Reform in Mexico: The Secretariat of Programming and Budget." *Interamerican Economic Affairs* 34, 1 (Summer): 27-60.

_________. 1984. "Public Budgeting in Mexico, 1970-1982." *Public Budgeting and Finance.* Spring.

Balassa, Bela, et al. 1986. *Toward Renewed Economic Growth in Latin America.* Mexico City: Colegio de Mexico.

Barry, Brian. 1985. "Does Democracy Cause Inflation? Political Ideas of Some Economists." In Lindberg and Maier, eds.

Bergsman, Joel. 1970. *Brazil: Industrialization and Trade Policies.* New York: Oxford University Press.

Bogdanwicz-Bindert, Christine A. 1985. "Small Debtors, Big Problems: The Quiet Crisis." Overseas Development Council, Policy Focus Series #5. Washington, D.C.: Overseas Development Council.

Bortz, Jeffrey. 1987. "The Dilemma of Mexican Labor." *Current History* 86, 518 (March).

Bouzas, Roberto, and Keifman, Saúl. 1985. "Argentina: El Plan Austral y las negociaciones financieras externas." *América Latina/Internacional* 2, 6 (October-December): 113-19.

Buffie, Eduard F., and Krause, Alan Sangines. 1987. "Economic Policy and Foreign Debt in Mexico." In Sachs, ed.

Cameron, David R. 1984. "Social Democracy, Corporatism, Labor Quiescence, and the Representation of Economic Interests in Advanced Capitalist Society." In *Order and Conflict in Contemporary Capitalism,* ed. John H. Goldthorpe. Oxford: Clarendon Press.

Camp, Roderic Ai. 1972. "The Middle Level Technocrat in Mexico." *Journal of Developing Areas* 6, 4 (July).

________. 1975. "The National School of Economics and Public Life in Mexico." *Latin American Research Review* 10, 3 (Fall).

Canitrot, Adolfo. 1980. "Discipline as the Central Objective of Economic Policy: An Essay on the Economic Programme of the Argentine Government since 1976." *World Development* 8, 11 (November): 913-28.

Cardoso, Eliana A. 1987a. "Inflation and Stabilization in Latin America: Orthodoxy versus Heterodoxy." Paper prepared for Conference on Stabilization Policy, Quito, Ecuador, October 1987.

________. 1987b. "Latin America's Debt: Which Way Now?" *American Economic Review* 77 (May).

Cardoso, Eliana, and Fishlow, Albert. 1988. "The Macroeconomics of the Brazilian External Debt." In Sachs, ed.

Caso-Raphael, Agustin, and Miranda, Jorge. 1979. *Política monetaria, inflación crecimiento económico: el caso de México.* Mexico City: Editorial Limusa.

________, and ________. 1984. "Patrones de política monetaria y gasto público en México. El desarrollo estabilizador." *El Trimestré Económico 51* (3), 203 (July-September): 591-614.

Cavarozzi, Marcelo. 1984. "Sindicatos y política y argentina." Centro de Estudios de Estado y Sociedad (CEDES).

________. 1986a. "Political Cycles in Argentina since 1955." In O'Donnell, Schmitter, and Whitehead, eds.

________. 1986b. "Peronism and Radicalism: Argentina's Transition in Perspective." *Working Paper* No. 170. Washington, D.C.: Latin American Program of the Wilson Center.

Cavarozzi, Marcelo; Riz, Liliana de; and Feldman, Jorge. 1986. "Concertación estado, y sindicatos en la Argentina contemporánea." Unpublished ms.; CEDES.

Chalmers, Douglas A. 1977. "The Politicized State in Latin America." In Malloy, ed.

Cohen, Benjamin J. 1986. "International Debt and Linkage Strategies: Some Foreign Policy Implications for the United States." In Kahler, ed.

Collier, David, ed. 1979. *The New Authoritarianism in Latin America.* Princeton: Princeton University Press.

Conjunctura Econômica. 1986. "O gigante volta às compras." July 15, p. 9.

Corro, Salvador, 1986. "En meteria economica, govierno y obreros en dirección contraria." *Proceso* 507 (July 21).

Crouch, Colin, 1986. "Conditions for Trade Union Wage Restraint." In Lindberg and Maier, eds.

Da Silva, Roque A. 1983. "Representatividade, democracia e unidade no sindicalismo brasileiro." *Coleção Cadernos* 1. Centro de Estudos de Cultura Contemporânea (CEDEA).

Diamand, Marcelo. 1978. "Towards a Change in the Economic Paradigm through the Experience of Developing Countries." *Journal of Development Economics* 5: 19-53.

Díaz-Alejandro, Carlos F. 1970. *Essays on the Economic History of the Argentine Republic*. New Haven: Yale University Press.

Dornbusch, Rudiger, 1984. "Argentina since Martinez de Hoz." National Bureau of Economic Research, *Working Paper* No. 1486. September.

Dornbusch, Rudiger, and De Pablo, Juan Carlos. 1987. "Debt and Macroeconomic Instability in Argentina." National Bureau of Economic Research.

Economist. 1987. "Economic Unit Intelligence Report: Argentina, No. 3."

Eichengreen, Barry. 1987. "Till Debt Do Us Part: The U.S. Capital Market and Foreign Lending." In Sachs, ed.

Escobar, Saul David. 1987. "Rifts in the Mexican Power Elite, 1976-1986." In Maxfield and Anzaldua M., eds., 65-88.

Eshab, Eprime, and Thorp, Rosemary. 1965. "Economic and Social Consequences of Orthodox Economic Policies in Argentina in the Postwar Years." *Bulletin of the Oxford Institute of Economics and Statistics* 27, 1 (February): 1-44.

Evans, Judith, and Bruce, James. 1986. "Fresh Faces in Third-World Finance." *Institutional Investor* (International Edition), September, pp. 167-72.

Evans, Peter. 1979. *Dependent Development: The Alliance of Multinational, State, and Local Capital in Brazil*. Princeton: Princeton University Press.

Faria, Hugo. 1986. "A Case Study of Macroeconomic Policy-making in a Crisis Environment: Brazil's Cruzado Plan and Beyond." Columbia University, School of International Affairs, Fall.

Felix, David. 1983. "On Financial Blowups and Authoritarian Regimes in Latin America." *Working Paper* #60 (October). Washington University, Department of Economics.

Fishlow, Albert. 1973. "Some Reflections on Post-1964 Brazilian Economic Policy." In *Authoritarian Brazil: Origins, Policies, and Future*, ed. Alfred Stepan. New Haven: Yale University Press.

_________. 1985. "The State of Latin American Economics." Stanford-Berkeley Occasional Papers in Latin American Studies.

Fitzgerald, E.V.K. 1978. "The State and Capital Accumulation in Mexico." *Journal of Latin American Studies* 10, 2 (November).

Foxley, Alejandro. 1980. "Stabilization Policies and Stagflation: The Case of Chile." *World Development* 8, 11 (November): 887-913.

_________. 1983. *Latin American Experiments in Neoconservative Economics.* Berkeley: University of California Press.

Foxley, Alexander, and Whitehead, Lawrence. 1980. "Economic Stabilization in Latin America: Political Dimensions." *World Development* 8, 11 (November).

Frenkel, Roberto, and Fanelli, José María. 1986. "Del ajuste caotico al Plan Austral." Centro de Estudios de Estado y Sociedad. June.

Frenkel, Roberto; Fanelli, José María; and Winograd, Carlos. 1986. "Stabilization and Adjustment Programs and Policies in Argentina." Centro de Estudios de Estado y Sociedad (CEDES).

Frenkel, Roberto, and O'Donnell, Guillermo. 1979. "The 'Stabilization' Programs of the IMF and Their Impacts." In *Capitalism and the State in U.S.-Latin American Relations,* ed. Richard Fagen. Stanford: Stanford University Press.

Frieden, Jeffry A. 1987. "The Brazilian Borrowing Experience: From Miracle to Debacle and Back." *Latin American Research Review* 22, 1.

_________. Forthcoming. "Debt, Development, and Democracy in Latin America: Classes, Sectors, and the International Financial Relations of Mexico, Brazil, Argentina, and Chile." *Comparative Politics.*

Garrido Noguera, Celso, and Quintana López, Enrique. 1987. "Financial Relations and Economic Power in Mexico." In Maxfield and Anzaldua M., eds., 105-26.

Gerschman, Silvia Victoria. 1985. "Representación y conflicto en dos formas de organización sindical: Comisión de Fábrica y Sindicato en el Brazil." *Working Paper* #38. Instituto Universitario de Pesquisas do Rio de Janeiro (IUPERJ), June.

Goncalves, Francisco Luiz Salles. 1985. "Duas vertentes e dois projetos no sindicalismo brasileiro." *Coleção Cadernos* #6. Centro de Estudos de Cultura Contemporânea (CEDEC).

Gourevitch, Peter. 1986. *Politics in Hard Times: Comparative Responses to International Economic Crises.* Ithaca: Cornell University Press.

Haggard, Stephan, and Kaufman, Robert. 1987. "The Politics of Stabilization and Structural Adjustment." In Sachs, ed.

Hansen, Roger D. 1971. *The Politics of Mexican Development.* Baltimore: Johns Hopkins University Press.

Herrera, Alberto Noriega. 1955. "Las devaluaciones monetarias de México, 1938-1954." *Investigación Económica (ENE) 15, 1: 149-77.*

Hewlitt, Sylvia Ann, and Weinert, Richard S., eds. 1982. *Brazil and Mexico: Patterns in Late Development.* Philadelphia: Institute for the Study of Human Issues.

Hinojosa, Oscar. 1986. "Banco de México y hacienda, manantiales de los hombres del presidente." *Proceso* 507 (21 July): 6-11.

Hirschman, Albert O. 1963. *Journeys Toward Progress: Studies of Economic Policy-Making in Latin America.* New York: Twentieth Century Fund.

_________. ed. 1961. *Latin American Issues: Essays and Comments.* New York: Twentieth Century Fund.

_________. 1981. *Essays in Trespassing: Economics to Politics and Beyond.* Cambridge: Cambridge University Press.

_________. 1985. "Reflections on the Latin American Experience." In Lindberg and Maier, eds.

Kahil, Raoul. 1973. *Inflation and Economic Development in Brazil.* Oxford: Oxford University Press.

Kahler, Miles, ed. 1986. *The Politics of International Debt.* Ithaca: Cornell University Press.

Katzenstein, Peter. 1986. *Small States in World Markets.* Ithaca: Cornell University Press.

Kaufman, Robert R. 1985. "Democratic and Authoritarian Responses to the Debt Crisis: Argentina, Brazil, and Mexico." *International Organization* 39, 3 (Summer): 477-81.

Keck, Margaret. 1986. "Great Expectations: The Worker's Party in Brazil, 1979-1985." Paper presented at the Latin American Studies Association convention, Boston, October.

King, Timothy. 1971. *Mexico: Industrialization and Trade Policies since 1940.* London: Oxford University Press.

Lamounier, Bolivar, and Mereguello, Rachel. 1986. "Partidos políticos e consolidação democrática: o caso brasileiro." Instituto de Estudos Econômicos, Sociais e Políticos de Saõ Paulo (INDESP).

Lara-Resende, André. 1984. "A moeda indexada: uma proposta para eliminar a inflação inercial." *Working Paper* #75, October. Departamento de Economia, Pontíficia Universidade Católica do Rio de Janeiro.

Lindberg, Leon N., and Maier, Charles S., eds. 1985. *The Politics of Inflation and Economic Stagnation.* Washington, D.C.: Brookings Institution.

Lindblom, Charles E. 1965. *The Intelligence of Democracy: Decision-Making through Mutual Adjustment.* New York: Free Press.

_________. 1977. *Politics and Markets: The World's Political and Economic Systems.* New York: Basic Books.

Lindblom, Charles E., and Braybrooke, David. 1963. *A Strategy of Decision: Policy Evaluation as Social Process.* New York: Free Press of Glencoe.

Lindblom, Charles E., and Dahl, Robert. 1953. *Politics, Economics, and Welfare: Planning and Politico-Economic Systems Resolved into Basic Social Processes.* New York: Harpers.

Lindert, Peter, and Morton, Peter. 1987. "How Sovereign Debt Has Worked." In Sachs, ed.

Lipson, Charles. 1986. "International Debt and International Institutions." In Kahler, ed.

Lopes, Francisco Lafaiete. 1984. "Inflação inercial hiperinflação e desinflação: notas a conjecturas." *Working Paper* #77, October. Departamento de Economia, Pontíficia Universidade Católica do Rio de Janeiro.

________. 1985. "Novo Austral na Argentina." *Working Paper* #104, July. PUC/Rio.

________. 1986. *A choque heterodoxo, combate à inflação e reforma monetária.* Rio de Janeiro: Editoria Campus Ltda.

Luna, Matilde; Tirado, Ricardo; and Valdes, Francisco. 1987. "Businessmen and Politics in Mexico, 1982-1986." In Maxfield and Anzaldua M., eds., 13-44.

Lustig, Nora, and Ros, Jaime. 1986. "Stabilization and Adjustment in Mexico, 1982-1985." Paper presented for the UNU/WINDER conference, Helsinki, August 19-21.

Mainwaring, Scott. 1986. "The Transition to Democracy in Brazil." *Journal of Interamerican Studies and World Affairs* 28, 1 (Spring): 149-80.

Mallon, Richard D., and Sourrouille, Juan V. 1975. *Economic Policy-Making in a Conflict Society: The Argentine Case.* Cambridge, MA: Harvard University Press.

Martins, Luciano. 1986. "The 'Liberalization' of Authoritarian Rule in Brazil." In O'Donnell, Schmitter, and Whitehead, eds.

Malloy, James M., ed. 1977. *Authoritarianism and Corporatism in Latin America.* Pittsburgh: Pittsburgh University Press.

Maxfield, Sylvia. 1986. "The Internationalization of Finance and Macroeconomic Management: Mexico and Brazil Compared." Paper prepared for the American Political Science Association meeting, Washington, D.C., August 27-September 1.

________. 1987. "Introduction." In Maxfield and Anzaldua M., eds., 1-12.

Maxfield, Sylvia, and Anzaldua M., Ricardo, eds. 1986. *Government and Private Sector in Contemporary Mexico.* Monograph Series #20. San Diego: Center for U.S.-Mexican Studies, University of California.

________. 1988. "National Business, Debt-led Growth and Political Transition in Latin America." In *Debt and Democracy in Latin America,* eds. Robert Kaufman and Barbara Stallings. Boulder, CO: Westview Press.

Medina, Luis. 1978. "1940-1952: Del Cardenismo al Avila-Camachismo." In Colegio de México, *Historia de la Revolución Mexicana*, vol. 18. Mexico City: Colegio de México.

Ness, Walter L. Jr. 1974. "Financial Markets as a Development Strategy: Initial Results from the Brazilian Experience." *Economic Development and Cultural Change* 22, 3 (April).

Noyola, J. 1956. "El desarrollo económico y la inflación en México y otros países latinamericanos." *Investigación Económica (ENE)* 16, 4: 603-6.

O'Conner, James. 1973. *Fiscal Crisis of the State.* New York: St. Martin's Press.

O'Donnell, Guillermo. 1973. *Modernization and Bureaucratic-Authoritarianism: Studies in South American Politics.* Berkeley: Institute of International Studies, University of California.

_________. 1977. "Estado y alianzas en la Argentina, 1966-1976." *Desarrollo Económico* 16, 64 (January-March).

_________. 1982. *El estado burocrático autoritario, 1966-1973: triunfos, derrotas y crisis.* Editorial de Belgrano.

O''Donnell, Guillermo; Schmitter, Philippe C.; and Whitehead, Laurence, eds. 1986. *Transitions from Authoritarian Rule in Latin America.* Baltimore: Johns Hopkins University Press.

Palomino, Héctor. 1986a. "El movimiento obrero y sindical en una larga transición." *El Bimestre* #26, pp. 12-21.

_________. 1986b. "Una imágen cualitativa de los conflictos laborales." *El Bimestre* #27, pp. 18-22.

Pastore, José, and Skidmore, Thomas E. 1985. "Brazilian Labor Relations: A New Era?" In *Industrial Relations in a Decade of Economic Changes*, eds. Harvey Jervis et al., 73-113. Madison, WI: Industrial Relations Research Association.

Payne, James L. 1965. *Labor and Politics in Peru: The System of Political Bargaining.* New Haven: Yale University Press.

Pellicer de Brody, Olga, and Mancilla, Esteban L. 1981. "1952-1960: El entendimiento con los Estados Unidos y la gestación del desarrollo estabilizador." In Colegio de México, *Historia de la Revolución Mexicana*, vol. 22. Mexico City: Colegio de México.

Purcell, Susan Kaufman. 1973a. "Authoritarianism." *Comparative Politics* 5 (January).

_________. 1973b. "Decision-making in an Authoritarian Regime: Theoretical Implications from a Mexican Case Study." *World Politics* 26, 1 (October): 28-54.

Randall, Laura. 1978. *An Economic History of Argentina in the Twentieth Century.* New York: Columbia University Press.

Reyna, José Luis, and Weinert, Richard S., eds. 1977. *Authoritarianism in Mexico.* Philadelphia: Institute for the Study of Human Issues.

Reynolds, Clark W. 1970. *The Mexican Economy: Twentieth Century Structures and Growth.* New Haven: Yale University Press.

Rivera Ríos, Miguel Ángel. 1985. *Crisis y reorganización del capitalismo mexicano, 1960-1985.* Mexico City: Ediciones Era, S.A.

Rock, David, ed. 1975. *Argentina in the Twentieth Century.* Pittsburgh: University of Pittsburgh Press.

Rogowski, Ronald. 1987. "Trade and the Variety of Democratic Institutions." *International Organization* 41, 2 (Spring).

Sachs, Jeffrey, ed. 1987. *Developing Country Debt.* Washington, D.C.: National Bureau of Economic Research, Inc., Conference Report. October.

Sandersen, Steven E. 1983. "Presidential Succession and Political Reality in Mexico." *World Politics* 35, 3 (April).

Schvarzer, Jorge. 1986a. "El estado en la gestión de Martínez de Hoz." *El Bimestre* #27, 3: 4-11.

_________. 1986b. "El estado y su mecanismo de regulación frente a diferentes situaciones macro-económicas." Paper prepared for CLASCO conference, Puerto Alegre, Brazil, July.

Serra, José. 1979. "Three Mistaken Theses Regarding the Connection between Industrialization and Authoritarian Regimes." In Collier, ed.

Sevares, Julio. 1986. "Los salarios en la Argentina." *El Bimestre* 26, 2.

Skidmore, Thomas E. 1967. *Politics in Brazil, 1930-1964.* London: Oxford University Press.

_________. 1977. "The Politics of Stabilization in Postwar Latin America." In Malloy, ed.

_________. 1979. "The Economic Dimensions of Populism in Argentina and Brazil: A Case Study in Comparative Public Policy." *New Scholar* 7, 1 & 2.

Skocpol, Theda. 1984a. "Emerging Agendas and Recurrent Strategies in Historical Sociology." In Skocpol, ed.

_________, ed. 1984b. *Vision and Method in Historical Sociology.* Cambridge: Cambridge University Press.

Smith, Peter H. 1979. *Labyrinths of Power: Political Recruitment in Twentieth Century Mexico.* Princeton: Princeton University Press.

Smith, William C. 1986. "The 'New Republic' and the Brazilian Transition?" Paper prepared for Latin American Studies Association meeting, Boston, October 23-26.

_________. 1981. *Economic Policy Reform in Mexico: A Case Study for Developing Countries.* Elmsford, NY: Pergamon.

Solis, Leopoldo. 1981. "Mexican Economic Policy in the Postward Period: The View of Mexican Economists." *American Economic Review* 61, 3 pt. supp. (June): 1-67.

Solnik, Alex, et al. 1987. *Porque no deu certo.* Sao Paulo: L&PM Editores, S.A.

Story, Dale. 1986. *Industry, the State, and Public Policy in Mexico.* Austin: University of Texas Press.

Suzigan, Wilson, et al. 1974. *Crescimento industrial no Brasil, incentivos e desempenho recente.* Rio de Janeiro: IPEA/INDES.

Thompson, John K. 1979. *Inflation, Financial Markets, and Economic Development: The Experience of Mexico.* Greenwich, CN: Jai Press.

Thorp, Rosemary, and Whitehead, Laurence, eds. 1979. *Inflation and Stabilization in Latin America.* New York: Holmes and Meier.

Torres, Blanca. 1984. "Hacia la utopía industrial." In Colegio de México.

Vasena, Adalbert Krieger, and Szewach, Enrique. 1985. "Inflation and Indexation: Argentina." In Williamson, ed.

Vernon, Raymond. 1965. *The Dilemma of Mexico's Development.* Cambridge, MA: Harvard University Press.

Villanueva, Javier. 1966. *The Inflationary Process in Argentina, 1943-1960.* Buenos Aires: Editoria del Instituto Torcuato di Tella.

Villarreal, René. 1984. *La contrarevolución monetarista: teoría, política, economía, e ideología del neoliberalismo.* Mexico City: Edicioines Océano S.A.

Viola, Eduardo, and Mainwaring, Scott. 1984. "Transitions to Democracy: Brazil and Argentina in the 1980s." *Working Paper* #21, July. Kellog Institute for International Studies.

Wallerstein, Michael. 1980. "The Collapse of Democracy in Brazil: Its Economic Determinants." *Latin American Research Review* 15, 3.

Wellons, Philip A. 1986. "International Debt: The Behavior of Banks in a Politicized Environment." In Kahler, ed.

Williamson, John, ed. 1985. *Inflation and Indexation: Argentina, Brazil, and Israel."* Washington, D.C.: Institute for International Economics. March.

Wirth, John D. 1970. *The Politics of Brazilian Development, 1930-1954.* Stanford: Stanford University Press.

Wynia, Gary W. 1978. *Argentina in the Postwar Era.* Albuquerque: University of New Mexico Press.

Zysman, John. 1983. *Governments, Markets, and Growth: Financial Systems and the Politics of Industrial Change.* Ithaca: Cornell University Press.

ROBERT R. KAUFMAN is a Professor of Political Science at Rutgers University. In recent years he has also been a Visiting Professor at Yale University and an associate of the Institute for Latin American and Iberian Studies at Columbia University. Recent publications by him include "Democratic and Authoritarian Responses to the Debt Crisis," "The Politics of Stabilization and Adjustment" (with Stephan Haggard), and *Debt and Democracy in Latin America,* co-edited with Barbara Stallings.

INTERNATIONAL AND AREA STUDIES

University of California at Berkeley

Richard M. Buxbaum, Dean

2223 Fulton Street, 3d floor — Berkeley, California 94720

Recent books published by International and Area Studies:

RESEARCH SERIES

80. *Beyond the Cold War: Conflict & Cooperation in the Third World.* Eds. George W. Breslauer, Harry Kreisler, & Benjamin Ward. $19.95
81. *Contemporary Catalonia in Spain and Europe.* Ed. Milton M. Azevedo. $13.50
82. *Liability for Negligence and Judicial Discretion.* 2d ed. Francesco Parisi. $18.50
83. *The Contradictory Alliance: State-Labor Relations and Regime Change in Mexico.* Ruth Berins Collier. $18.50
84. *The Future of European Security.* Ed. Beverly Crawford. $23.50
85. *High Technology and Third World Industrialization: Brazilian Computer Policy in Comparative Perspective.* Eds. Peter B. Evans, Claudio R. Frischtak, & Paulo Bastos Tigre. $14.95
86. *The New Portugal: Democracy and Europe.* Ed. Richard Herr. $15.50
87. *Russia and Japan: An Unresolved Dilemma between Distant Neighbors.* Eds. T. Hasegawa, J. Haslam, & A. Kuchins. $26.50
88. *Political Parties in Russia.* Ed. Alexander Dallin. $10.95
89. *European Dilemmas after Maastricht.* Eds. Beverly Crawford & Peter W. Schulze. $22.95
90. *The Soldiers' Story.* Heinämaa, Leppänen, and Yurchenko, eds. $12.50

EXPLORATORY ESSAYS

1. *The Question of Food Security in Cuban Socialism.* Laura J. Enríquez. $7.50

INSTITUTE OF INTERNATIONAL STUDIES

POLICY PAPERS IN INTERNATIONAL AFFAIRS

38. *Vanguard Parties & Revolutionary Change in the Third World: Soviet Perspectives & Their Implications.* David E. Albright. $9.50
39. *Lessons of the Gulf War: Ascendant Technology and Declining Capability.* Gene I. Rochlin and Chris C. Demchak. $5.50
40. *Impediments on Environmental Policy-Making and Implementation in Central and Eastern Europe: Tabula Rasa vs. Legacy of the Past.* Peter Hardi. $6.50
41. *Flying Apart? Japanese-American Negotiations over the FSX Fighter Plane.* Gregory W. Noble. $7.25

42. *Beware the Slippery Slope: Notes Toward the Definition of Justifiable Intervention.* Ernst B. Haas. $6.50

INSIGHTS IN INTERNATIONAL AFFAIRS SERIES

1. *Confrontation in the Gulf: University of California Professors Talk about the War.* Ed. Harry Kreisler. $7.95
2. *Refugees: A Multilateral Response to Humanitarian Crises.* Sadako Ogata. $5.95
3. *American Intervention after the Cold War.* Robert W. Tucker. $3.95
4. *Crisis in the Balkans.* Eugene A. Hammel, Irwin M. Wall, & Benjamin N. Ward. $6.95

CENTERS FOR SOUTH & SOUTHEAST ASIA STUDIES

MONOGRAPH SERIES

32. *Scavengers, Recyclers, & Solutions for Solid Waste Management in Indonesia.* Daniel T. Sicular. $16.50
33. *Indonesian Transmigrants and Adaptation: An Ecological Anthropological Perspective.* Oekan S. Abdoellah. $14.95
34. *Thai Music and Musicians in Contemporary Bangkok.* Pamela Myers-Moro. $22.50
35. *In the Shadow of Change: Images of Women in Indonesian Literature.* Tineke Hellwig. $22.00

OCCASIONAL PAPERS SERIES

15. *The Penis Inserts of Southeast Asia: An Annotated Bibliography with an Overview & Comparative Perspective.* Donald E. Brown, J. W. Edwards, & R. P. Moore. $6.00
16. *Patterns of Migration in Southeast Asia.* Ed. Robert R. Reed. $19.50
17. *Bridging Worlds: Studies on Women in South Asia.* Ed. Sally J. M. Sutherland. $17.50
18. *Essays on Southeast Asian Performing Arts: Local Manifestations and Cross-Cultural Implications.* Ed. Kathy Foley. $14.95

LANGUAGE TEACHING MATERIALS

Devavanipravesika: Introduction to the Sanskrit Language. Robert P. Goldman & Sally J. Sutherland. $23.50

Teaching Grammar of Thai. William Kuo. $23.50

Tamil for Beginners, 2 vols. Kausalya Hart. $12.50 ea.